COLLAGE
LOST AND FOUND

giuseppina "josie" cirincione

NORTH LIGHT BOOKS

NORTH LIGHT BOOKS
CINCINNATI, OHIO
WWW.ARTISTSNETWORK.COM

GIUSEPPINA (JOSIE) CIRINCIONE sells her unique, artistic jewelry and cards at specialty boutiques in the Phoenix, Arizona, area. She designs samples and stamps for Stampotique Originals. Josie enjoys taking art classes from her local college, and at the Phoenix Center for the Arts. As a master of ephemera, she also packages found collage materials, for sale at local stamp stores. She considers her education in the creation of art as a never-ending one and is always discovering ways to take her own art in new directions.

11 10 09 08 07   6 5 4 3 2

Distributed in Canada by Fraser Direct
100 Armstrong Avenue
Georgetown, ON, Canada L7G 5S4
Tel: (905) 877-4411

Distributed in the U.K. and Europe by David & Charles
Brunel House, Newton Abbot, Devon, TQ12 4PU, England
Tel: (+44) 1626 323200, Fax: (+44) 1626 323319
Email: mail@davidandcharles.co.uk

Distributed in Australia by Capricorn Link
P.O. Box 704, S. Windsor, NSW 2756 Australia
Tel: (02) 4577-3555

Library of Congress Cataloging-in-Publication Data

Cirincione, Giuseppina.
  Collage lost and found : creating unique projects with vintage ephemera / Giuseppina "Josie" Cirincione.
    p. cm.
  Includes index.
  ISBN-13: 978-1-58180-787-5 (pbk. : alk. paper)
  ISBN-10: 1-58180-787-2 (pbk. : alk. paper)
  1. Collage. I. Title.
  TT910.C5 2006
  702'.81'2—dc22
                                        2005028275

EDITOR: **TONIA DAVENPORT**
DESIGNER: **KARLA BAKER**
PRODUCTION COORDINATOR: **GREG NOCK**
PHOTOGRAPHERS: **AL PARRISH, TIM GRONDIN AND CHRISTINE POLOMSKY**
PHOTO STYLIST: **JAN NICKUM**

fw F+W PUBLICATIONS, INC.

METRIC CONVERSION CHART

TO CONVERT	TO	MULTIPLY BY
INCHES	CENTIMETERS	2.54
CENTIMETERS	INCHES	0.4
FEET	CENTIMETERS	30.5
CENTIMETERS	FEET	0.03
YARDS	METERS	0.9
METERS	YARDS	1.1
SQ. INCHES	SQ. CENTIMETERS	6.45
SQ. CENTIMETERS	SQ. INCHES	0.16
SQ. FEET	SQ. METERS	0.09
SQ. METERS	SQ. FEET	10.8
SQ. YARDS	SQ. METERS	0.8
SQ. METERS	SQ. YARDS	1.2
POUNDS	KILOGRAMS	0.45
KILOGRAMS	POUNDS	2.2
OUNCES	GRAMS	28.3
GRAMS	OUNCES	0.035

DEDICATION

To my parents, Giuseppe and Francesca, for keeping their traditions alive, and to my brother Guiseppe, for having two of the most beautiful girls, Bella and Vita.

ACKNOWLEDGEMENTS

First of all, thanks to Jim and Carol of Stampotique Originals. If I hadn't walked into their store a few years ago, I would not be publishing this book. They are the ones who introduced me to North Light Books and Christine Doyle, the managing editor. Thank you for believing in me and for taking this project to its completion. I would like to thank Tonia Davenport for pushing me into the twenty-first century and adding the Internet to my list of tools. Her constant guidance throughout this process was incredibly valuable. Much gratitude goes to Christine Polomsky for all the step-out photos and my hand-modeling job. Thank you to everyone at North Light Books, for making the process so enjoyable.

TABLE OF CONTENTS

FASHION **FORTISSIMO** 84
(HOME ACCESSORIES • JEWELRY • GIFTS)

WHAT'S OLD IS NEW

When I was little, I was always making something. I remember cutting pictures out of magazines and gluing them onto different surfaces, or I would use my mom's sewing scraps to make little dolls. I was always searching around the house for things I could use. This kept me busy for hours.

Several years ago, I thought it would be fun to make my own thank-you cards. The techniques I was using as a kid, I am still using now. The main difference is the subject matter (and the fact that I can now use power tools and sharp scissors). What I did for fun then, has turned into my favorite form of expression now.

Inspiration, for me, comes from two places: my family and the bygone era that they lived in, before I came along. I was raised in a Sicilian household, and the Italian language has been a part of my everyday life. I enjoy bringing its words and phrases into my work. My family has always loved keeping a record of their lives and experiences with photographs, and it is oftentimes one of these photos that jump-starts a new piece of art for me. The stories I've been told that accompany the photos make starting even easier.

Because of my passion for the past, I have been dealing with vintage antiques (primarily those of the 1930s to the 1960s) for the past eleven years. During this time, I have amassed quite a collection of ephemera, game pieces, photos and sewing notions. I even live in a 1940s bungalow and the interior is furnished with original 1950s furniture. It is from these things and this environment that I find creative expression a breeze.

Your inspiration could come from a black-and-white photo of your favorite aunt. The background you create for a collage from this inspiration could be something as simple as a page from an old book, and you could add your favorite color from an inkpad or an old button that reflects your aunt's style. Every object you decide to add leads you in another direction.

What I like most about collage is that you can express yourself using not just colors of paint or paper but a variety of textures, images and found objects.

As you will see in this book, collage is not limited to canvas or an assemblage in a box. It can be used in jewelry, cards, handmade books and journals too. The possibilities are endless, so don't be afraid to experiment! My hope is that this book gives you insights into expressing yourself through collage and teaches you new techniques to incorporate in your own work. Remember, at the end of the day, this is something to do for fun, for the pure enjoyment of creative expression (and maybe to breath new life into an object that otherwise would have been forgotten).

PHOTOS, FOUND OBJECTS AND THE MISCELLANEOUS
(GOOD PLACES TO FIND STUFF)

I go thrift shopping and antiquing just about every day of the week. Beware; it's addicting! Searching for collage materials, the interesting people you meet along the way and the history behind the objects you find is all part of the process. The best part is that you don't have to spend a lot of money. A twenty-five-cent trinket could end up being the focal point of your project.

The places I frequently visit include thrift stores, antique stores, estate sales, yard sales, dollar stores, hardware stores, office supply stores, the Internet and my friends and family.

I have lived in Phoenix most of my life but have been fortunate enough to have traveled quite a bit. I have visited flea markets throughout the United States and Europe. Flea markets are most often seasonal or monthly and they attract hundreds of dealers from all over the country, so you can imagine all the unique treasures that converge in one place. One of the best ways to find flea market locations is on the Internet. Magazines such as *Mary Engelbreit's Home Companion* and *Martha Stewart Living* sometimes offer feature stories on different flea markets as well.

One great venue opportunity I stumbled upon was a vintage postcard show. There's one held in Phoenix once a year that consists of tables and tables covered with boxes and boxes of vintage postcards, photos, game pieces and paper ephemera. When I walked into the room, I had to pinch myself! I couldn't believe there was so much variety and selection in one space. The show was overwhelming for a first-timer like me, but after eight hours of rummaging through boxes, I left with bags full of goodies and an open-arm invitation to come back next year. The dealers at that show (and most dealers in general) were quite knowledgeable. If you're ever at a show and you don't see what you're after, just ask. You'll be surprised by what they have stashed under their tables. I recall one charming 82-year-old dealer who had quite the collection. He even had vintage, hand-tinted postcards from Italy. Check the Internet for postcard or other specialty shows in your area.

Another tip to keep in mind as you build your found object collection: More eyes mean even more great stuff; let your friends know what you are looking for so they can be on the lookout as well. My friend Beth is always gathering and hunting for unique pieces of ephemera that I can use in future projects.

The things I am drawn to over and over again fall under the category of family and heritage. I look for Italian words, phrases and old typefaces, along with memorabilia that reminds me of family abroad and before my time (such as pinup girls of the 1950s).

Whenever my parents go back to Sicily, all I ask is that they bring back old family photos. A great way to personalize your own work is to use family photos, letters, a birthday card, charms from Aunt Rosetta's old bracelet, etc. Anything that has personal meaning. Be sure to photocopy or scan your photos or any original ephemera you wish to preserve. Sometimes you will want to use the original itself in a piece, but more often than not, if your original item is paper, you can safely store the original and put a color or black-and-white copy to work in your collage.

I encourage you to keep your eyes open, wherever it is you go, for items you can use in collage. The objects and themes that interest you have probably been right under your nose all along, you just haven't seen them as elements for collage. Begin searching for these elements with new eyes.

COLLAGE WITH WHAT?
(SUPPLIES, MATERIALS AND FINDING EPHEMERA)

Here are some of the basic supplies you will need to get started. Most of these basic craft supplies you probably already own—if not, you can find them at your local craft, stamp, art supply or hardware store. Experiment with different things. The items listed here are among my favorites, but you may find that something different works better for you.

CARDSTOCK

Cardstock is great for its stability and provides an easy way to add color. Whenever possible, I like to use found paper items, such as old packaging or postcards. If using new card-stock, I prefer at least an 80-lb. (170gsm) weight.

PAINT

I don't spend a lot of money on paints. Sometimes I use them for a basecoat of color, but I mainly use them watered down, as washes. I like to use craft-grade acrylics that come in 2oz. (59ml) plastic bottles.

INKPADS AND REINKERS

When using rubber stamps, black is my ink color of choice, and my two favorite brands are StazOn and VersaFine (both by Tsukineko). They both create a dense, opaque image. I also use inkpads to create background colors. The transparent layers mix to add depth and dimension, and they will not cover the text completely. I use ink from the reinker bottles like paint or as a glaze to antique items. Be sure to use permanent reinkers.

ADHESIVES

For adhering paper to paper, I like to use a double-sided adhesive such as Tombo Mono Adhesive. Aleene's Tacky Glue is a good all-purpose adhesive for attaching small embellishments (I like to work with it from a small paint palette, and thin it with a bit of water. You can then apply it with a small brush.) You can use paper glaze as a glue or a sealant to add dimension. Gel medium works as an adhesive or a sealer, and you can also mix it with paint to change the texture. I prefer to use matte gel medium on my projects; I like the finish and its light texture better than the glossy variety.

LEAFING PENS

Leafing pens are paint pens that make it so easy to add bits of gold or silver to your work. I use them to finish off the edges of many projects. They come in a variety of metallic colors and different tip sizes.

MARKING PENS

A permanent black pen (such as a Sharpie) is my marker of choice, and I use it to color the edges of many paper pieces before adhering them to my collages. This gives them definition and distresses them a bit at the same time. This type of marker is also used to color the sides of a domino in the domino pendant project (page 86). A variety of colored pens is nice to have on hand just for adding small touches of color, or to touch up desired areas on occasion.

EYELETS

Eyelets come in a variety of sizes, shapes and colors. They attach papers together, add texture and dimension and give a finished look to punched holes. To use these handy embellishments, you'll need an eyelet setter and most often a hammer.

EMBELLISHMENTS

So many items can be used as embellishment in your collage work. Small bits of paper ephemera (postage stamps, doily pieces, images cut from vintage advertisements and so on), beads, spirals of wire or tiny charms (milagros)

are just some of the things you can use as a finishing touch. One of my favorite ways to embellish a piece is to add tiny shapes, such as stars punched from colored cardstock, using a decorative paper punch.

COPPER FOIL TAPE

Copper foil tape is designed to edge pieces of glass and conduct heat, so the pieces of glass can be soldered together. It is available in a variety of widths and different colored backs. If used in the proper width, you can use it to bind two pieces of glass together with a thin collage sandwiched between them. It also works well as a decorative element. You can produce an aged look on it with liver of sulfer, a patina or StazOn reinkers and it can also be embossed with metal letter markers (see the album project on page 66).

FLUX

Flux is used with copper tape as an adhering agent for solder. I prefer to use Sterling Flux; it's available at your local hardware store or from a stained-glass retailer.

SOLDER

Solder is what gives a finished, metallic beaded edge to foil-wrapped pieces such as the slide and glass marble jewelry projects on pages 96–117. It comes coiled on a spool in different thicknesses. I prefer to use either solid wire solder or Thin Ultimate decorative solder, sold at stained glass stores.

WIRE

I use wire in quite a few projects. It comes in different types and gauges. The smaller the gauge number, the thicker the wire. I like to use 18-gauge aluminum wire for my jewelry findings and black 28-gauge annealed steel to bind books and journals, to adhere found objects and as an embellishment. Experiment with different gauges and wire types; it is an inexpensive way to add another element to your work.

STUDIO ESSENTIALS
(STANDARD TOOLS TO HAVE ON HAND)

Most of the items listed here are basic craft tools that you can find at your local craft or stamp store. If you have been crafting for a while, you probably have many of these items already.

RUBBER STAMPS

Stamps provide a great way to add text, color and images to your work. They work well for creating a layered effect or to add interest to any background. The number of alphabets and images that you can purchase is immense and, with all of the different types of inks that are available, you can stamp on any surface from paper to glass to metal.

DUSTER BRUSH

I like to use duster brushes (sometimes referred to as stipple brushes) to add color or an antique effect to many different surfaces. When using one of these brushes with an inkpad, be sure to blot your brush on a piece of scrap paper before applying ink to your artwork. Use a light hand and start with lighter colors. Darken as you go, applying a heavier coat of the lighter colors or progressing to darker shades until you achieve the look you want.

METAL LETTER STAMPS

Metal letter stamps come in different fonts and sizes. These are great for adding debossed text to any background. If you want to highlight specific words, use the stamps along with a contrasting ink color. Or, for a more subtle look, don't use any ink.

DECORATIVE PUNCHES

Decorative punches are good tools to have on hand for adding interest to a background or to draw the eye to your main image. There are many shapes (dots, leaves, squares and so on) and sizes available. I find myself frequently using tiny stars and hearts. By using a punch, I can cut out a lot of them quickly and easily.

ANYWHERE PUNCHES

The name says it all. Handheld punches work fine but can be limiting in that they won't reach beyond a certain point. Anywhere punches allow you to pierce holes *anywhere* you desire. They come in different sizes and are often sold with a small hammer in a kit.

SCISSORS

Invest in a good pair of scissors. Collage work demands a lot of cutting. I prefer Fiskars brand. For detailed work, use small, fine-tipped scissors to get clean and accurate cuts.

EYELET SETTER

Eyelet setters are used to secure eyelets to your collage elements. Most require the use of a hammer and a protective surface such as a cutting mat. Some versions will set an eyelet with just a single push and no hammer, but I haven't tried that type. Setters come in different sizes; choose according to the size eyelet you wish to secure.

CRAFT KNIFE

Craft knife blades come in a variety of sizes; I primarily work with a no. 11 blade. For a straight, clean line, use them along a hard edge, such as a metal ruler. They offer the best way to cut out details from the interior of an image as well. Being frugal with your craft blades (i.e., trying to work with one that's dull) can backfire on you and shred a wonderful image—always work with a sharp blade.

CUTTING MAT

A self-healing cutting mat isn't just great for cutting on; if you purchase one that is large enough, it makes a great work surface as well, protecting your worktable from ink smears and glue globs.

ANYWHERE PUNCH

METAL LETTER STAMPS

ACRYLIC RULERS

These transparent rulers have a multitude of applications and come in several lengths and widths. C-Thru makes a ruler that has a metal edge on it that's perfect for cutting paper with a craft knife. I love using the acrylic rulers made for quilters as well because they are wide and their grid pattern makes sizing a snap. The transparent quality of any acrylic ruler allows you to see what you are cutting.

LABEL MAKER

Label makers make adding text and a bit of color to your projects superquick and easy. Label tapes come in different sizes and a variety of colors. You can buy them at your local office supply stores but I find most of mine at local garage sales and thrift shops. Even though the tape comes backed with adhesive, I like to apply craft glue to smaller bits to ensure long-term staying power.

JEWELRY PLIERS

Round-nose pliers are used to make jump rings, spirals and loops. Jewelry wire cutters are used to snip wire, and flat-nosed pliers are used to open and close a jump ring. To make the jewelry in this book, you will need all three on hand. Jewelry pliers are easy to find in the beading section at most craft stores.

SOLDERING IRON

Soldering irons are used to melt and spread solder. Be sure to purchase one that is at least 30 watts or higher. There are different types and styles available; find one that is comfortable for you. I like to use the most basic type, which is sold at hardware stores—you don't need to spend a lot of money to get a great tool.

Using your iron takes practice and patience. Don't get frustrated with yourself if your first result is less than perfect, and remember, imperfections add character to your overall project.

NYLON BRUSHES

For many craft applications, a variety of brushes will do the job, but when it comes to layering on glue or paper glaze as a sealer, a flat nylon brush produces the fewest visible brushstrokes. Nylon brushes are easy to recognize by their white or sometimes color-dyed bristles. Choose the appropriate size for your project.

HOT POT

I have dedicated a small Crock-Pot for the use of heating beeswax. If you plan to work with beeswax, you'll need a slow cooker or craft hot pot for melting the wax. Beware: The wax gets very hot so don't try to spread it with your fingers—I learned the hard way. Slow cookers are frequently found at yard sales or thrift shops.

ACCESS TO A COLOR COPIER

I have become a fixture at the photocopier in my neighborhood quick-print store. Making color copies is an easy way to preserve your images. They allow you to preserve your old photos and ephemera, and the copies inherit the intrinsic quality of an aged piece of paper or an old photo. I make color copies of everything unless I am going to use an image to make a transfer or if a black-and-white image simply works better for my project (in either case, a standard laser or toner-based copy works best). You can also use a color copier to alter the color and size of your images, a wonderful tool when just a bit smaller or larger would be ideal.

He knew at the first sight of her that it was a happy day

Subject
Date

la·dy-kill·er, n. (Slang), a man ... are supposed to be irresistibly att[...]

LET US MAKE A DUPLICATE OR COLOR
PRINT FROM THIS TRANSPARENCY

"Do you promise?"
she asked. "Yes, my sweet,"
he whispered. "I will always
be here at your side."

DELAWARE
JOSIE
4 2 3
3 1 7 6 1

lu·mi·nous

cards
in·vi·ta·tion·s
jew·el·ry
etc.

COLLAGE CATECHISM

(GREETING CARDS / TAGS / BUSINESS CARDS)

THE OXFORD DICTIONARY defines collage as a picture formed by fixing various items to a background, while HyperDictionary.com describes it as a paste-up made by sticking together pieces of paper or photographs. (*A paste-up*—I like that.) I realize that you already are well aware of *what* a collage is, but you may be asking things like: *where* do I start, *what* size should it be or *how* can I make my work unique? I hope this chapter clears up many of your questions quickly. You'll want to get a handle on the basics and become comfortable with collage right away because there is much more fun to be had throughout the rest of the book, and I can't wait to share it all with you.

When I first began playing with collage, I started making cards and tags because I considered their sizes "friendly." Filling a 5" x 7" (13cm x 18cm) card is not as intimidating as trying to fill up a blank 8" x 10" (20cm x 25cm) canvas. Going small is also a good way to explore different techniques and compositions, and to find the supplies that work

best for you. Besides, it's fun making something, such as a card, to send to someone else because you get to share a piece of yourself.

The collaged business cards, also in this section, came about out of necessity. I was going to order the run-of-the-mill black-and-white sort that come in a box of 500 from the local office supply store, but I felt they really did not represent what I do. Collage is a format that can work well for many artists' business cards because it compiles elements that best represent the aspects of you and your work.

We'll start this section with building a basic collage, and you'll see that it does not take a closet full of found objects or a full spectrum of paints to complete a pleasing and expressive piece of art. One of my favorite architects, Mies van der Rohe, said, "Less is more." It's not a surplus of clutter, but rather well-chosen items that will best suit your project.

WHAT GOES WHERE?

(GETTING STARTED WITH COLLAGE)

SO YOU'VE COLLECTED ALL THIS STUFF and your scissors are sharpened. Now what? If you've never tackled collage before, I suggest you start simple. It doesn't take a lot of elements to make a successful composition. Start with a few handpicked things that you love and remember that there's more than one right way to place things.

A greeting card for a friend is the perfect excuse to practice collage. Don't wait for a special occasion—think of your collage as a "just because" gift in and of itself. As you can see from the examples on pages 22–25, your stories can take you as far as you want to go.

BASIC NEEDS

- **color copies of your favorite photos**
- **found paper for background choices**
- **detail-cutting scissors**
- **smaller ephemera**
- **double-sided adhesive**
- **craft glue**
- **paint palette**
- **fine brush** (for gluing)
- **recycled novels** (for cutting out text)
- **cardstock in color of your choice**
- **craft knife**
- **small decorative punch** (optional)

Suppose we join hands It yet remains to see

Spotlight Dance
Vira Boys Ass'n, Inc.

SAT EVENING FEB 9

hidden treasure

When I was little, I loved receiving letters from my grandparents in Sicily, who sent their notes tucked inside these colorful envelopes. Don't assume you will only find inspiration from a photo or pretty postcard. Sometimes it's the most simple pieces of ephemera that trigger the best memories.

CHECKERS & BACKGAMM

1. Trim the excess paper away from your color-copied photos, so it's easier to play around with them and to find a pleasing composition.

2. Select different backgrounds to consider.

3. Hold different photos over the assorted backgrounds until you find something that clicks.

4. When you have decided on the photo and background you want to use, trim the subject itself from the rest of the photo using detail-cutting scissors.

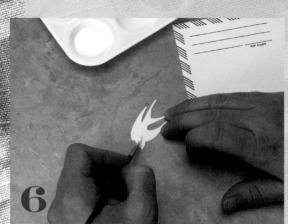

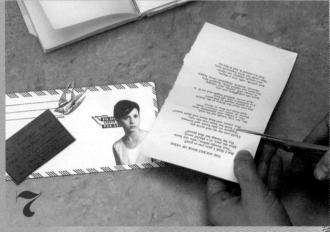

5. Choose other elements to tell your story, selecting items that look good together. Then start playing with composition. Attach larger elements with double-sided adhesive.

6. For smaller elements, pour some craft glue onto a paint palette and apply it to the paper with a fine brush. (This might be easier if you thin the glue with just a bit of water.)

7. You'll find great text in old novels. Purchase several from the used book store or a garage sale so you will always be able to find just the right words.

8. Sometimes I will adhere the small bits of cut-out text to a piece of cardstock and then trim the individual words just to give the text some definition.

9. Arrange the text over the collage and, after you've placed the words where they look best, adhere them using a fine brush and craft glue. Use the tip of a craft knife to both pick up and move around the text.

10. As you adhere your elements, your collage begins to take shape and it becomes easier to visualize whether or not you would still like to add additional elements. Sometimes all that's needed is a few tiny details, like hearts punched out of cardstock with a decorative paper punch.

FOR THIS CARD, I COMBINED VINTAGE LACE, PUNCHED-OUT DYMO LETTERS AND PHOTO CORNERS. THE BACKGROUND IS VINTAGE HAIR NET PACKAGING, AND I HAND-COLORED THE BABY IMAGE WITH COLORED PENCILS. THIS WAS ONE OF MY FIRST COLLAGE CREATIONS!

THE BACKGROUND LAYER IMMEDI-
ATELY BEHIND THE SAILOR GIRL
INCLUDES A NOTIONS CARD, WITH
ORIGINAL SNAPS STILL IN PLACE,
ATOP AN ENDEARING HEART.
I LOVE HOW THE LITTLE GIRL
SEEMS TO BE SEARCHING THE
HORIZON FOR A CLUE TO HER
HEART'S DESIRE.

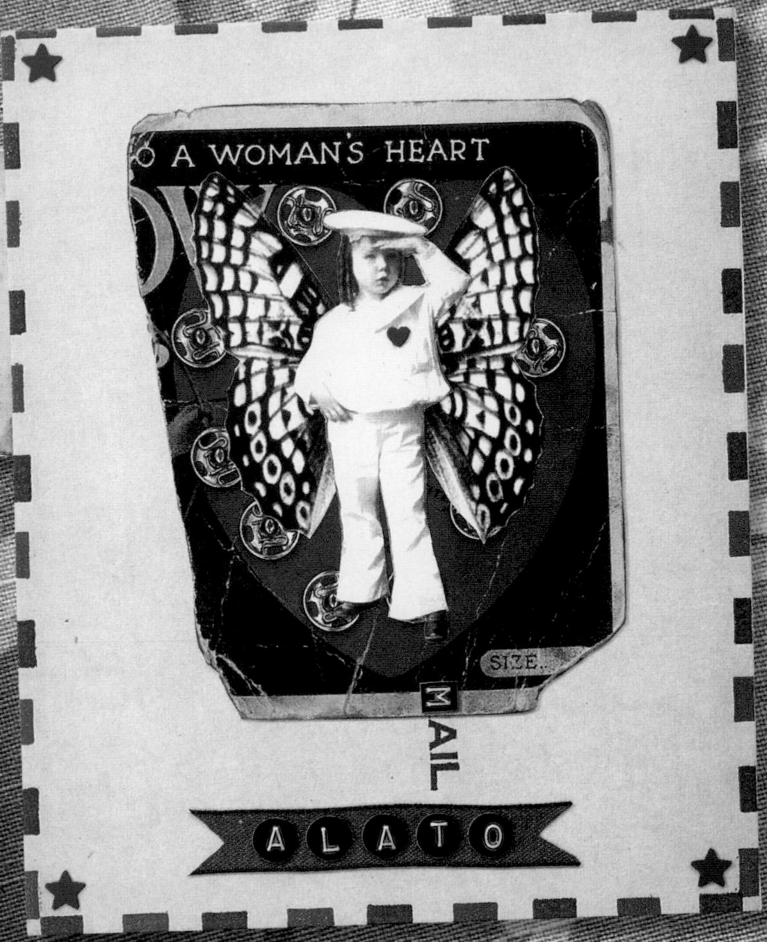

O A WOMAN'S HEART

M AIL

A L A T O

LEICA
M6

You never looked lovelier,
Miss Elliott.

5

276

CHARLEY

I IMAGINE THIS GENTLEMAN
CALLER TO BE PEERING
LONGINGLY THROUGH THE
LENS OF THE CAMERA AT THE
WOMAN. I CHOSE THIS PHOTO
OF A WOMAN BECAUSE OF
HER PROTECTIVE COMPANION
AND HIS SPIKED COLLAR.

"GOLD MEDAL"   De Luxe EDITION

Implements for Playing

CKERS & BACKGAMM

COPYRIGHT MCMXLV BY TRANSOGRAM COMPANY, INK, NY

ROMA
Stadio Olimpico
Olimpic Stadium
Stade Olimpique
Olimpik Stadium
Estadio Olimpico

May 4

Here we are in Rome, + enjoying

The sea is his

MY DAD, "SAILOR JOE," WAS IN
THE ITALIAN NAVY, AND YOU WILL
SEE HIM AS AN INSPIRATION IN
SEVERAL OF THE PIECES IN THIS
BOOK. IT WAS NICE HAVING AN OLD
ITALIAN POSTCARD AVAILABLE TO
USE AS THE BACKGROUND.

THIS PIECE STARTED WITH AN ANTIQUE
MAGAZINE AD FOR A PRAM. THE DIC-
TIONARY TEXT COVERING THE SLIDE
FRAME LENDS UNEXPECTED WHIMSY,
WHICH MAY HAVE GONE UNNOTICED
HAD I NOT HIGHLIGHTED A SPECIAL
TERM WITH THE TINY RED HEART. A
FINAL TOUCH OF RIBBON ADDED A
PRETTY TEXTURE.

baby buggy

LLOYD STREAMLINED
PRAM — No. 4860. Exclu-
sive design in modern sty-
ling—offering new standards
of comfort.

CARRIAGES
FOR '48!

Different! The Newest
Variety in Canada

23

crux de collage

If you're not sure if your piece is done, leave it for a while and come back to it. If you like it, it's done! If you don't like it, continue adding elements one at a time. I subscribe to the less-is-more theory.

He knew at the first sight of her that it was a happy day

THE ROMANCE OF A WEDDING DAY WAS THE PERFECT EXCUSE TO USE VINTAGE LACE THAT I FOUND AT AN ANTIQUE STORE. ALTHOUGH THE ROSE IN THE BOTTOM CORNER IS A STICKER, IT MATCHES PERFECTLY WITH THE ROSES ON THE VINTAGE CARD BACKGROUND.

24

egyptian twilight dance

LUX
COFFEEBAR
4404 N. CENTRAL
266 ★ 6469
★
SUNDAY 7 PM
MAY ★ 16th

One Sweetly Solemn Thought.

I CREATED THIS INVITATION FOR A FRIEND
WHO WAS HOSTING A BELLY DANCE PER-
FORMANCE. AN EVENING EVENT, THE
SPACE HAD AN OLD-WORLD-MORROCAN
FEELING, SO I TRIED TO PLAY THAT UP
WITH THE COLLAGE.

Try Your Luck
1¢ to 89¢
PAY WHAT YOU PUNCH
FROM 1¢ to 89¢, NO HIGHER
EVERY PUNCH WIN

25

IT'S ALL A GAME
— CAPICHE?
(WORKING WITH A SURFACE YOU LOVE)

IF YOU DON'T LOVE THE SURFACE you start with, chances are, you're not going to be starry-eyed over the finished product. And while winning the war on creation is great, why not enjoy the entire game? It warrants repeating—start with what you love. I love starting a collage with a vintage bingo card. Each card has a unique patina, and the fonts for the letters and numbers typically go well with the images I like to use. Many local stamp stores now carry vintage bingo cards. Other great places to look are antique malls and the Internet. While I am turned on by bingo cards, antique catalog pages may be what get you going.

THE JUXTAPOSITION OF THE OLD WORLD (FROM A HANDCOLORED TOURIST'S POSTCARD) WITH A 1950s PINUP PRODUCES A FUN CONTRAST. BESIDES, I COULDN'T RESIST USING THIS IMAGE FOR ITS BULLET BRA (THE STARS ARE A PERSONAL ADDITION).

he said, cocking his head, "you have a lot of spark for a woman!"

hidden treasure

Find a surface that speaks to you, and if it's something that you can find time and time again, make a series like the assortment of bingo cards I have here. You will often find that dealers repeatedly carry the same items, so try returning to the dealer who first sold you an item before hunting all over town; chances are, the dealer may have a fresh assortment of what you're looking for.

ALTHOUGH MY MOM IS INDEED ANGELIC, FOR THIS CARD, I GAVE HER BUTTERFLY WINGS. THE ADDITIONAL BUTTERFLY AT THE BOTTOM PROVIDES BALANCE TO MOM'S IMAGE, BUT ITS SUBTLE SOFTNESS DOESN'T UPSTAGE HER.

I LIKE TO USE SLIDE COVERS AS A FRAME WITHIN A LARGER PIECE. IT CREATES ANOTHER STORY WITHIN THE OVERALL COMPOSITION. A PIECE OF MICA BETWEEN THE SLIDE AND THE IMAGE OF THE WOMAN'S HEAD AND HOUSE ADDS JUST A BIT MORE COLOR AND HELPS SEPARATE HER HEAD FROM THE BINGO CARD BACKGROUND.

BINGO

District Number 2

Stockbridge
Madison Co. N.Y.

Spring Term 1900.

PRESENTED BY
Ethelyn R. Cooke,
TEACHER.

OFFICERS

Daniel Trew
Martin Fitzpatrick
Elmer Trew

lady-love, n. a sweetheart.

BINGO

BINGO

DOROTHY DIX

KODACHROME
TRANSPARENCY

KODACHROME TRANSPARENCY

38	47	64
59	70
30	73
31	57	67
34	52

13

7

When Contemplating Matrimony, Girls, Don't Marry Your First Sweetheart; Don't Be Taken In By the Lure of Forbidden Fruit Married Men Often and Shut Your Door to All Appeals From Lame Ducks

WELCO

The "Big Store are invited to desire. A free anything sent

II PARIS — La Tour Eiffel

I CHOSE THIS PICTURE BECAUSE THE COUPLE IS REALLY HAPPY AND LOOKS LIKE THEY DESERVE TO CHASE A DREAM. I TRIMMED THE STARS THAT OVERHUNG THE EDGE OF THE CARD BUT LEFT A SINGLE BUTTERFLY WING UNTRIMMED TO DRAW YOUR EYE TO THE COUPLE.

THE INSPIRATION FOR THIS CARD CAME OUT OF MY FIXATION FOR THE 1950s—FAST CARS, GLAMOROUS GIRLS AND A BROWNIE CAMERA THAT USED THOSE FUNNY BLUE BULBS.

crux de collage

Not all of your elements have to fit entirely within the confines of the background surface. It makes things more interesting to have parts of some elements run off the edge.

I TRIMMED THE STAR ON THE BUL-
LET BRA TOP OF THE CORSET IN AN
ATTEMPT TO KEEP THE PERSPECTIVE
TRUE TO FORM. THE OBVIOUS CON-
TRAST BETWEEN THE TWO PRIM AND
PROPER WOMEN AND THE UNDERGAR-
MENT IMAGES WAS HUMOROUS TO
ME, SO I HAD EVEN MORE FUN WITH
THE TEXT.

FOR THIS CARD, I CHOSE A POKER
BINGO CARD BECAUSE IT WORKS WELL
WITH THE PINUP GIRL IMAGE. THE
GIRL APPEARS COY IN HER STRAW
HAT, AND I THOUGHT SHE MIGHT NEED
"SPECIAL HANDLING."

STARRY-EYED

(INCORPORATING RUBBER STAMPS)

YOU DON'T HAVE TO USE IMAGES CUT FROM
BOOKS OR MAGAZINES to create collage. Rubber-stamped
images are a great alternative. I search for images that are reminiscent
of the period and style of photos and ephemera I like to use. One of my
favorite stores, Stampotique Originals, uses actual photos to create some
of their rubber stamps. The image for this card is straight out of 1950s
Brooklyn. It reminds me of one of my favorite movies, *The Lords of Flatbush*.

BASIC NEEDS

background paper to stamp on
  (ideally, something perforated
  or that has been punched for a
  coil binding)

Distress inkpads
  (TIM HOLZ-RANGER):
  Black Soot
  Tea Dye
  Walnut Ink

duster (stipple) brush

Courting rubber stamp
  (STAMPOTIQUE ORIGINALS)

black inkpad
  (VERSAFINE)

heat gun

cardstock

slide cutter
  (or craft knife, ruler and
  cutting mat)

scoring attachment for
slide cutter
  (or bone folder and ruler)

bone folder

black permanent marker

pencil

1/16" (2mm) anywhere punch

hammer

cutting mat

Vintage Script rubber stamp
  (STAMPOTIQUE ORIGINALS)

needle

colored thread of your choice

decorative punch

label maker

cellophane envelope
  (to mail card)

1. First choose a paper that you want to rubber-stamp on. You don't always have to use plain, solid paper. Here, I am using a piece from an old bridge score pad that I found at an antique booth. Distress your paper using distress inkpads and a duster or stipple brush. I like to use a variety of colors together.

2. To use a large rubber stamp, tap it over a raised inkpad. I like to use black.

3. After the stamp is well-inked, press it onto your paper. It is easier to stand up and put your weight into it.

4. Swiftly lift up the stamp and voilá!

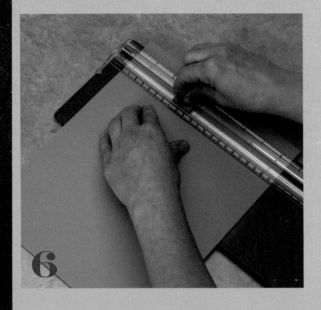

5. Heat-set the ink with a heat gun so you don't have to wait for it to dry.

6. Trim cardstock for your card to a size that is compatible with the envelope you will be using. I like to use a slide cutter because it's quick and easy.

7. Score the card down the center using either the slide cutter and the scoring attachment or a ruler and a bone folder. Then fold the card and crease it with the bone folder.

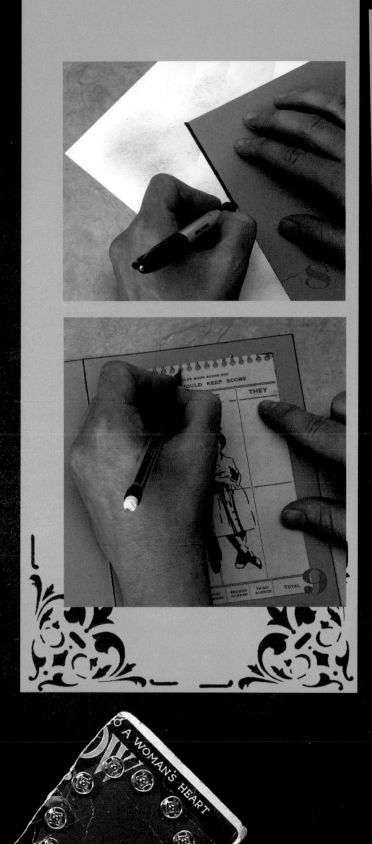

8. Edge the card to give it some definition by going around the outside with a black permanent marker.

9. A cool way to attach the stamped image to the front of the card is to sew it. For this card, I'm going to sew along the perforated edge of the paper. First, mark where the punched holes are with a pencil.

10. Punch out the holes using an anywhere punch and a hammer, over a cutting mat. Here, I used a $1/16"$ (2mm) punch.

crux de collage

Address your card on the back of the card itself, then insert it into a clear cellophane envelope to mail. Your recipient can view your work the moment it arrives!

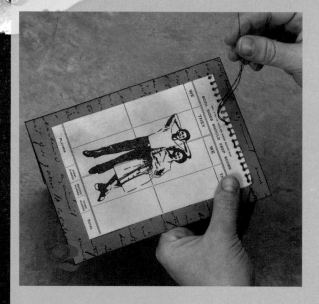

11

13

11. Before sewing on your stamped image, you may want to first distress the card front using the duster brush and distress inks. Use script or other background stamps to add interest to the background of the card.

12. Using a needle and four strands of thread (in a contrasting color from the paper), sew the stamped image to the top of the card through the prepunched holes.

13. Add tiny embellishments, such as stars punched from a sheet of cardstock. An easy way to create your own text is by using an old-fashioned label maker. Punch out your words, peel and stick.

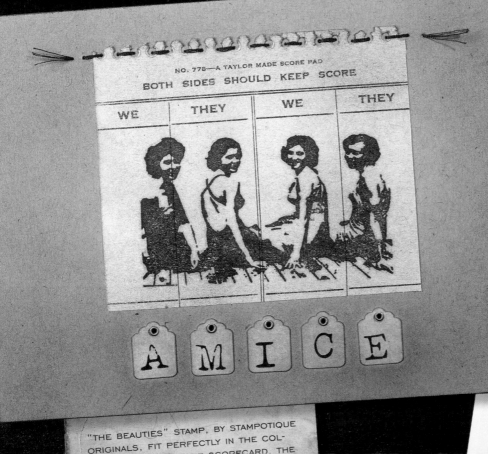

NO. 776—A TAYLOR MADE SCORE PAD

BOTH SIDES SHOULD KEEP SCORE

WE	THEY	WE	THEY

A M I C E

"THE BEAUTIES" STAMP, BY STAMPOTIQUE
ORIGINALS, FIT PERFECTLY IN THE COL-
UMNS OF THIS VINTAGE SCORECARD. THE
TINY TAGS AT THE BOTTOM ARE ACTUALLY
STICKERS BY A COMPANY CALLED NOSTAL-
GIQUES. I ADDED THE EYELETS TO GIVE
THE APPEARANCE OF AUTHENTIC TAGS.

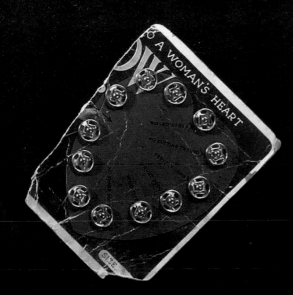

A WOMAN'S HEART

THIS IMAGE OF THE COUPLE (FROM THE GREAT DEPRESSION ERA SERIES BY STAMPOTIQUE ORIGINALS) WAS STAMPED ONTO A VINTAGE FILE CARD AND ATTACHED AT THE SIDES WITH A BACKSTITCH AND BLANKET STITCH— YOU NEVER KNOW WHAT SORT OF COOL ELEMENTS YOU CAN INCOORPO-RATE FOR COLOR AND TEXTURE.

FOR THIS CARD, I PLAYED WITH EXAG-
GERATED PROPORTION FOR EMPHASIS
AND COMPOSITION. THIS IS AN EXAMPLE
OF HOW SOME IMAGES ARE STAMPED
AND CUT OUT, AND SOME IMAGES ARE
LEFT STAMPED ON THE BACKGROUND. I
PUNCHED AND CUT THE NUMBERS AND
STARS FROM RAFFLE TICKETS.

BEHIND CLOSED DOORS
(USING EMBOSSING POWDER)

IF YOU LIKE TO INCORPORATE RUBBER STAMPS into your collage work, further enhancing the images with embossing powder is a perfect way to add texture and color. Available in a large number of colors, plus clear, this powder requires the use of a heat gun to melt it. Experiment with different combinations of pigment ink and powders. This is also a good way to sneak metallics into your work.

1. Stamp your image onto a piece of paper using either embossing ink or a pigment ink. While the ink is still wet, sprinkle on your chosen embossing powder.

2. Tap off the excess powder onto a sheet of scrap paper, then funnel the excess powder back into the jar.

3. Heat the image with a heat gun to melt the powder. The result is a raised, glossy image.

4. This image can be used as a window for another image. To create the window, cut out the outside shape with scissors, and then use a craft knife and cutting mat to cut out the interior shapes.

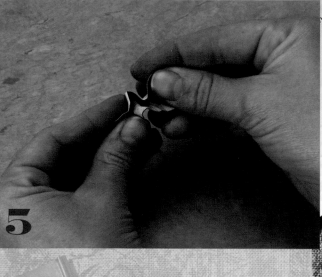

5. Distress the embossed image further with a duster brush and distress inks. Because the inside of the "shutters" will be visible on this image as well, I've also distressed the backs of the doors. Use a paper towel to wipe the ink off the embossed areas. Add color to the image with markers. Set the window aside. Crumple up a second image to show behind the window.

6. Distress the crumpled image with ink using the duster. Layer the embossed window over the crumpled image using double-sided tape. Stamp the script stamp onto cardstock, then sprinkle on gold embossing powder and heat to melt. Layer the window image onto the script background, then adhere the paper to the front of the card.

crux de collage

A fun way to layer your images onto the front of the card is to use small snaps. After creating a stamped background for the window image, punch holes in the four corners of the background piece, using a $^1/_{16}$" (1mm) hole punch. Now just put the back of the snap inside of the card, insert the raised portion through the hole and snap on the front part to secure.

COMBINED, THESE STAMPED IMAGES (INVOKE ARTS) ARE LARGE ENOUGH TO BE ABLE TO COMPETE WITH THE BOLD COLOR OF THE BINGO CARD. METALLIC EMBOSSING POWER PROVIDED A MORE ETHEREAL EFFECT FOR THE ANGELIC SUBJECT.

THE CHOSEN THREE

(CREATING FAUX SHEET METAL)

METAL REPAIR TAPE IS ONE OF THOSE THINGS
that I found while browsing the aisles of the hardware store. It's designed
to repair metal air ducts. Because it comes in a tape form, it is pliable and
soft. It's also easy to distress; you can punch holes through it, stamp on
it, paint on it and you can use it to hinge a book because it doesn't tear. It
has a strong adhesive back. To stain the metal, I like to use reinker inks
because of their transparent quality. Be sure to use permanent inks.

BASIC NEEDS

piece of trimmed matboard
approximately 4" x 6"
(10cm x 15cm)

metal repair tape
(found in hardware stores,
used to repair ductwork)

bone folder

sandpaper or sanding block

damp paper towel

black reinker bottle
(STAZON)

paint palette

duster (stipple) brush

Timber Brown reinker bottle
(STAZON)

Henna reinker bottle
(ANCIENT PAGE)

Sienna reinker bottle
(ANCIENT PAGE)

found or decorative paper
(for background of stamped
image)

Summer of '32 stamp
(STAMPOTIQUE ORIGINALS)

number stamps

black inkpad
(VERSAFINE)

1. Trim a piece of mat board to the size you will want the metal layer to be. Cover one side and the edges with strips from the roll of metal repair tape.

2. Burnish the tape down with a bone folder. Burnish the sides as well.

3. Go over the tape with sandpaper or a sanding block. I like to use emery blocks from the beauty supply store because they're very inexpensive.

4. Wipe off the sanding dust with a damp paper towel. Make multiple dents in the tape with your fingers or fingernails. Squeeze some ink from the reinker onto the palette. Apply ink to the foil using a duster brush. Work the color in well with the brush.

5. If you've applied too much color, go back with the sandpaper and sand some of it off. Repeat with Henna, Timber Brown and Sienna inks.

6. Stamp images onto a found paper of your choice (I used a piece of sheet music, here, and stamped with the Summer of '32 stamp and three numbers.) Layer the stamped paper over the metal tape to cover the center, exposed area of the mat board. Add additional elements, such as the hooks I used, if you wish.

RATHER THAN USING THE MINIMAL
AMOUNT OF TAPE REQUIRED TO FILL
THIS CARD, I CHOSE TO OVERLAP
THE STRIPS SEVERAL TIMES. THE
VERTICAL LINES THAT RESULTED CRE-
ATE MOVEMENT THAT FOLLOWS THE
FAN OF THE RUNNING ATHLETES. BY
KEEPING THE NUMBER OF COLORS
USED TO A MINIMUM, I MADE THE
COMPOSITION MORE DRAMATIC.

HERE, I USED METAL LETTER PUNCHES TO
ADD DEPTH TO THE BACKGROUND. I LIKE
HOW THE SNAPS IN THE CORNER APPEAR
TO REPEAT THE IMAGE OF THE MUSCLE
MAN'S BARBELL. THE ELONGATED STYLE OF
THIS CARD ENHANCES THE STRENGTH OF
THE TOWERING WOMAN.

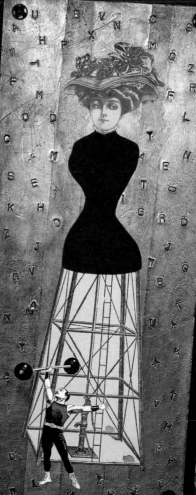

DOES IT COME
IN A SMALLER SIZE?
(ADAPTING COLLAGE TO A SMALLER SCALE)

ARE YOU THINKING YOU MIGHT NOT ALWAYS HAVE THE GUMPTION TO FILL THE SPACE OF A STANDARD GREETING CARD? I certainly feel that way sometimes! Collage is definitely not a one-size-fits-all art form. I like to create art in some shape or form at least once a day just to keep my creative muscle toned. Smaller surfaces such as a tag, index card or coaster are opportunities to get a quick collage fix.

What do you do with a tag? It's ideal as a hang tag for a special gift, or you can tie on a pretty ribbon for a bookmark. You can laminate one and use it as a luggage tag, bind several together for a tag booklet or use one as an embellishment on a larger collage piece. So many ways to use a tag!

BASIC NEEDS

standard shipping tag

paper for background
 (can be found paper)

glue stick

craft knife

cutting mat

black paper or cardstock

½" (13mm) circle punch

¼" (6mm) hole punch

black permanent marker

color copy of a
black-and-white photo

watercolor pencils
 (optional)

clear packing tape
 (3M Super-Strength)

bone folder

small tub of water

paper towel

collage materials of your choice

hidden treasure

Found papers such as old maps, sheet music, or recipe-of-the-month cards all serve as great background options for creating a tag collage. Because the overall size of a tag is relatively small, it's easy to have a single piece of ephemera fill the entire space. Even paper that you might not normally consider inspiring becomes an intriguing part of your collage story.

ADAPTING A SURFACE PAPER TO A TAG SHAPE

One of the easiest ways to work with a surface paper that you like in a small format is to mount it onto a shipping tag. This is as easy as one-two-three.

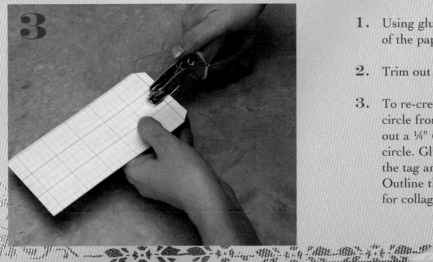

1. Using glue stick, adhere one side of the tag to the back of the paper of your choice.

2. Trim out the tag using a craft knife and a cutting mat.

3. To re-create a hole protector, punch out a ½" (13mm) circle from cardstock, using a circle punch, then punch out a ¼" (6mm) hole from the center of the punched circle. Glue the punched circle to the top center of the tag and repunch the center hole through the tag. Outline the tag using a black marker. It is now ready for collage elements of your choice.

ADDING A TAPE TRANSFER TO YOUR COLLAGE

A tape transfer is an interesting way to add transparent layering to your collaged tags or to any collage art. Start with standard clear packing tape. If the image you wish to transfer is wider than the roll of tape, nestle one piece of tape next to another until the image is covered in tape or use a large roll of contact paper.

1. To create a tape transfer, start with a black-and-white copy of a photograph. You can add color to the photograph using colored pencils, if you wish.

2. Apply a strip of clear packing tape over the part of the image you wish to use. Here, I don't wish to transfer the entire photograph, just an important part of the image.

3. Burnish the tape to the image using a bone folder. Rub in multiple directions. Be sure there are no bubbles.

4. Immerse the taped image into a tub of water. Leave it in the water for a couple of minutes or until the paper is completely saturated.

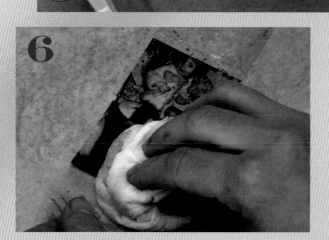

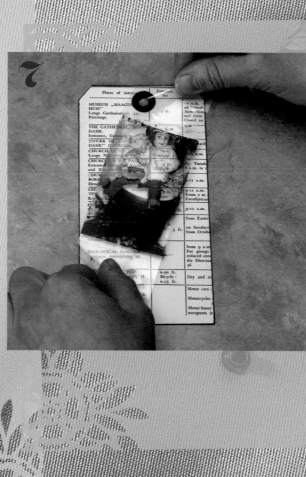

5. Begin rolling off the paper from the tape. Rub it with your fingers gently until all of the paper is gone and you can see through the tape.

6. Blot the excess water off of the tape with a paper towel.

7. The tape is still sticky, so you can stick it right onto your collage.

Mi piace questa città.

ITALY

IF YOU HAD A PHOTO OF YOUR MOM AND DAD RIDING A VESPA IN ITALY DURING THE 1950s, YOU WOULD USE IT IN YOUR COLLAGES TOO!

Bellezza

BELLEZZA TRANSLATES TO BEAUTY. THAT ABOUT SUMS IT UP, DON'T YOU THINK? I USED RUBBER STAMPS OVER LEDGER PAPER FOR THE BACKGROUND AND HAND-COLORED THE BLACK-AND-WHITE PHOTO OF THE CAR WITH COLORED PENCILS.

SOME DAYS YOU LOSE YOUR HEAD, BUT YOU FIND A PRETTY ROSE INSTEAD, AND EVERYTHING JUST COMES TOGETHER, LIKE THIS LITTLE HANG TAG.

The golden hours on angel wings Flew o'er my dearie; For dear to me as light and life, Was my sweet Highland Mary

To those who go, And those who come; Good-bye, proud world! I'm going home.

THE BACKGROUND OF THIS CARD IS A COMBINATION OF AN OLD ENVELOPE, PART OF AN ATLAS AND A STRIP OF NUMBERS. EXPERIMENT WITH DIFFERENT COMPOSITIONS WHEN CREATING YOUR BACKGROUNDS.

I USED METAL REPAIR TAPE AS THE BACKGROUND FOR THIS TAG TO SHOW THE DIVERSITY OF THIS MATERIAL. I USED STAZON INK TO STAMP THE NUMBERS, AND THE METAL FOIL STARS ARE THE SAME ONES I GOT FROM MY TEACHERS WHEN I DID GOOD WORK IN SCHOOL.

THIS IS A GREAT EXAMPLE OF LAYERING. IN THIS ONE TAG ALONE, I HAVE USED RUBBER STAMPS, A PAPER SLIDE COVER, AN EMBOSSED RUBBER-STAMPED IMAGE, AN OLD PHOTO, SCRAPBOOK PAPER, DYMO WORD LABELS, TINY BUTTONS AND HAND-SEWING.

MAY I GIVE YOU MY COLLAGE?

(USING COLLAGE TO PROMOTE YOURSELF)

If you thought business cards came only from the printer, think again. By making your own, you not only get to make each one a true work of art, you also don't have to wait for an order to come in. Be as creative as you like with this project; consider the possibility of a folded card, a transparency or a recycled shopper's card.

These cards will not get lost in the shuffle or tossed out of the Rolodex! Keep the original as your master and make color copies on heavy cardstock. Rounding the corners is optional, and if you have too much text to use a label maker, print the text from your computer, then cut and paste it creatively.

BASIC NEEDS

background texture or image
(photocopied onto
heavy-weight cardstock)

corner rounder
(optional)

label maker

¼" (6mm) hole punch

craft glue

collage elements of your choice
(including small text cut
from a book)

hidden treasure

Because business cards are typically printed in multiple quantities, you don't have to worry about finding original ephemera for each and every card. Create one original collage that combines interesting images and found items, then scan the original and print out copies of it for the cards you will be handing out. Depending on the quantity you want and your particular home printer, it may be less expensive to have a copy house make the copies.

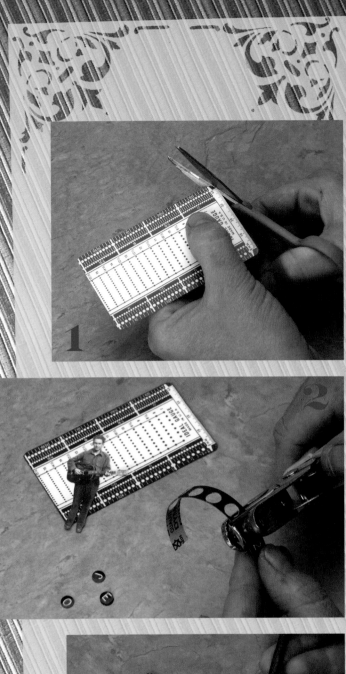

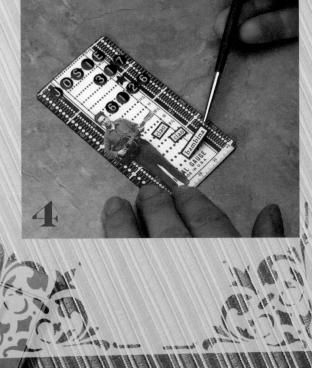

1. Photocopy a background for your card onto heavy-weight cardstock. Trim the card down to business card size: 2" x 3½" (6cm x 9cm). Round the corners, too, if you like.

2. Punch out letters using a label maker to spell your text, leaving a space between each letter. Then punch out each letter with a ¼" (6mm) hole punch.

3. Glue the letters onto the card using craft glue. Glue on additional elements as well.

4. In addition to the business info, you can also add smaller text to complete the collage composition.

USING A LABEL MAKER AND A HOLE PUNCH, THE EXTRUDED LETTERS BECOME MORE INTERESTING THAN TRADITIONAL LABEL STRIPS. THE TAPE IS AVAILABLE IN A VARIETY OF COLORS FOR JUST THE RIGHT PUNCH!

I REALLY LIKE THE LOOK OF LICENSE PLATES AS A BACKGROUND, AND THEIR ROUNDED CORNERS MADE TRIMMING THE CARDS EASY. FOR YOUR OWN VERSION, COPY A PLATE ON THE COLOR COPIER, AND REDUCE ACCORDING TO YOUR OWN PREFERENCE.

THE BACKGROUND OF THIS CARD IS COMPOSED OF A TAPE TRANSFER FOR THE SIGNING HANDS (DOVER CLIP ART) ADHERED TO A PAGE FROM AN OLD MAGAZINE.

FOR THIS CARD, I ADDED DIMENSION BY USING DYMO LABELS, JOLEE'S DIE-CUT FLOWERS AND AN IMAGE OF A BOUDOIR GIRL. THE HANDWRITTEN TEXT FROM THE ORIGINAL POSTCARD ADDS A BIT OF CHARM AS WELL.

I MODIFIED THE CLIP ART HAND BY REMOVING THE BIRD ORIGINALLY PERCHED ON THE FINGER AND REPLACING IT WITH AN IMAGE OF A LITTLE MAN, TO ADD A BIT OF SURREALISM.

A FORMAL VIEWING

(BOOKS / SHRINES / WALL ART)

WHEN YOU EXPRESS YOURSELF THROUGH COLLAGE (or any art form), you consciously and subconsciously leave behind small clues to the stories long forgotten in the depths of your private mind. Oftentimes when you've completed a collage, you want to share your story with others. There are many ways to show off your masterpieces and, let's face it, collage is meant for display. Collage work on canvas or paper easily slides into a frame. Have you thought of setting out a book whose cover has been altered? And we are all intrigued by the sight of a shrine, which invites the viewer to take a look inside.

With the basics understood, it's easy to take your collage skills a step further by blending techniques to create more substantial pieces. Don't be afraid to explore the possibilities of different materials; at the core of collage lies experimentation and finding new applications for supplies and elements. In this section, we will explore two-dimensional and three-dimensional approaches.

I love to find old, distressed frames and cut them down to new sizes that suit my needs, but you can start with any frame you love and create a piece of art to fit it, if you're not into cutting it down. Shrines need not be limited to cigar boxes—how about using a wine box, an old jewelry box or a small fruit crate? Or think outside the box altogether and come up with your own creative display solutions.

59

BOOK OF SECRETS

(CREATING AN "OLD" BOOK FROM SCRATCH)

GASKET MATERIAL IS ANOTHER ITEM that just seemed to pop off the shelf when I was in search of inspiration at the hardware store. It is perfect for book covers, since durability is important. Strong and easily distressed, gasket material comes in a roll, accepts color nicely and remains flexible and malleable.

Unlike duct tape, gaffer's tape is made of cloth but has the same strength and staying power. It's also easy to write on and comes in a few different colors. I prefer black for binding books and finishing off edges. This product is used in the film industry and can be found easily online if there's not a set and lighting supply store in your area.

BASIC NEEDS

matboard
(enough to make front and back covers, the size of your choice)

craft knife

ruler

cutting mat

gasket material
(found in hardware stores)

double-sided adhesive

scissors

black inkpad
(StazOn)

Sienna inkpad
(Ancient Page)

paper towel

duster brush
(optional)

gaffer's tape

sandpaper

found or decorative paper
(for the inside of front and back covers)

1/16" (2mm) anywhere punch

hammer

1/16" (2mm) long eyelets

eyelet setter

cardstock
(enough to make pages for the book — they will be folded in half)

pencil

heat gun
(optional)

28-gauge annealed steel or aluminum wire

wire cutters

assorted beads

collage material for the front cover

1. Using a craft knife, a ruler and a cutting mat, trim two pieces of matboard to the size you wish to have your book covers, and a piece for the spine as well.

2. Trim one piece of gasket material so it's ½" (13mm) larger on all sides than each of the cover pieces (not the spine). Crumple up the pieces, working them in your hands until they are fairly soft and pliable. Apply double-sided adhesive to one side of one cover. Smooth out a piece of the crumpled paper and adhere the board to the paper, centering it.

3. Use scissors to notch out the corners.

4. Wrap the paper around the board, securing it to the back of the board with more double-sided adhesive. Repeat for the other half of the cover. Using the black StazOn (or permanent) inkpad, rub color over the front of each covered piece.

5. Repeat with the Sienna inkpad and wipe off the excess ink with a paper towel. (Use a duster brush to add additional spot color, if desired.)

6. Use gaffer's tape to wrap the edges of the cover pieces. The tape should extend over the front of the cover about ¼" (6mm).

7. Using scissors, trim the excess tape that extends beyond the ends of the cover.

8. To connect the spine to the covers, set a piece of tape sticky side up between the two covers, so the tape extends ¼" (6mm) onto the backs of the covers. Center the spine onto the tape (there should be about ³/₁₆" [5mm] of space between either side of the spine and the covers).

9. Wrap the excess around to the front, and trim so they are even with the edges of tape around the covers.

10. Center another piece of tape over the front of the spine.

11. Wrap the edges around to the inside. Work the cover, folding it back and forth to work in the tape around the spine.

12. Sand the taped edges of the cover to knock down the shine. (If any white shows through the tape, go over it with the duster brush using the black inkpad.)

13. Trim some found paper of your choice to cover the insides of the front and back covers (about ⅛" [3mm] smaller than the cover). You may wish to decorate the paper with rubber stamps or colored pencils, or you can collage it with images. Adhere the papers to the inside of each half of the covers with double-sided adhesive.

14. Using a ¹⁄₁₆" (2mm) anywhere hole punch, punch three holes down the center of the spine.

15. Insert a long eyelet through the front of each hole.

16. Turn the cover over. Using an eyelet setter and hammer, set the eyelets from the inside of the cover.

17. Trim or tear eight to ten pieces of a paper to the size of the unfolded cover less ⅛" (3mm). Fold the pages in half and stack them together to form a signature. You may wish to trim the inner two or three pieces a bit if they look like they will extend beyond the edge of the cover when they are folded and sewn into the book.

18. Center one piece of folded paper in the cover, and use a fine pencil to mark the holes through the eyelets. With the 1/16" (2mm) anywhere punch, punch holes at the marks on the fold. Use this as a template to punch the remaining pages. (You can punch 2–3 sheets at time.)

19. Dip the edges of each sheet into a pigment inkpad. I like to use either red or black. Set aside to dry or dry it with a heat gun.

20. Trim about 1 yard (91cm) of 28-gauge annealed steel wire and use it to sew the pages to the cover. Go through each hole a couple of times, ending with the wire ends on the outside.

21. Add a second, shorter piece of wire in order to have one piece of wire coming out of each of the three holes, weaving the ends through the rest of the wire to secure them. Trim the excess wire off, on the inside.

22. Thread beads onto each wire, and wrap each wire end to finish. Embellish the front of the book as desired.

ALBUM DI FAMIGLIA

(EMBELLISHING A BOOK WITH METAL)

AS A GIFT FOR A FRIEND, a blank book with a custom cover is personal, plus it encourages your friend to fill the pages. I chose the sheet metal tape to bind the book because once distressed, it has the look of galvanized steel. I used metal slide mounts to frame the photos and chose copper tape to add the words with metal letter stamps. Metal slides are tricky to find; check old photo supply houses, antique stores or the Internet. As an alternative, see the project on page 69 for which I used paper slide mounts as frames. You could also spray paper mounts with metalic paint or cover them with metal repair tape.

BASIC NEEDS

matboard
(enough to make front and back covers, the size of your choice)

craft knife

ruler

cutting mat

metal repair tape
(found in hardware stores, used to repair ductwork)

bone folder

sandpaper

black inkpad
(StazOn)

Timber Brown inkpad
(StazOn)

paper towel

1/8" (3mm) anywhere punch

1/16" (2mm) anywhere punch

hammer

1/8" (3mm) eyelets

eyelet setter

paper for interior pages
(slightly smaller than the back cover piece)

19-gauge annealed wire

wire cutters

found or decorative paper
(for the inside of front and back covers)

metal slide mounts

images to show through the slide mounts

scissors

cardstock
(to back the images)

double-sided adhesive

copper tape

metal letter stamps

decorative brads

craft glue

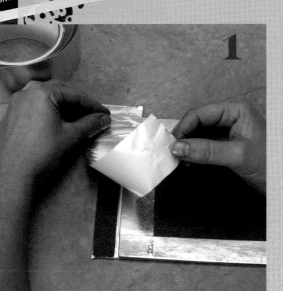

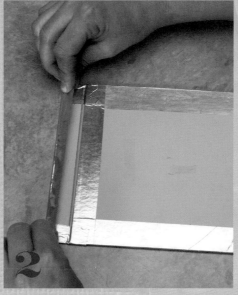

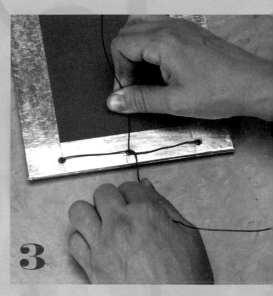

1. Trim two pieces of matboard for the covers (consider the number of slides you are going to want to use to determine size). From one of the pieces of board, cut ¾" (2cm) off of one short side for the spine, using a craft knife, ruler and a cutting mat. Cover the edges of both cover pieces with metal repair tape. Burnish the tape down with a bone folder. Set the front cover and spine piece on top of the back cover to check for placement of the spine piece (there should be 3/16" gap). Attach the spine to the front cover with a strip of metal repair tape.

2. Turn the cover over, wrap the tape around and burnish with a bone folder. Cut a second strip of the metal tape and apply to the inside of the cover.

3. Distress the metal tape with sandpaper, and black and Timber Brown ink (see steps 3–5, pages 43–44). Punch three ⅛" (3mm) holes in the spine on the front cover. Using those holes as a template, punch corresponding holes in the back cover. Set eyelets in each of the holes (see steps 14–16, page 64). Sand the eyelets to take some of the paint off. Cut or tear paper for the interior pages and punch holes in one end, using a cover as a template. Sew the covers and pages together with about 2' (61cm) of 19-gauge annealed wire. Twist the wire together in the center at the back.

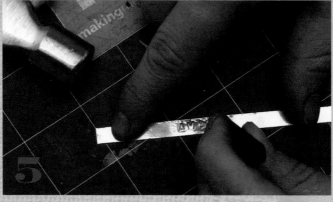

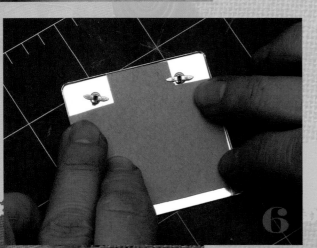

4. Trim the wire with wire cutters and hit with a hammer to flatten. Trim paper of your choice to cover the inside of the covers. Select the first image for a slide mount. Trace around the outside of the mount, over the chosen part of the image.

5. Cut out the image with scissors and adhere to a piece of cardstock using double-sided adhesive. Cut the image out of the cardstock. Sand the slide mount to distress it a bit, and add StazOn black ink. Stamp out the title for your mount in copper tape, using metal letter stamps and a hammer. Here, I am spelling the Italian word (*amico*) for *friends*.

6. Rub black StazOn ink over the lettered tape, then wipe off excess ink with a paper towel. Trim the tape, leaving enough on either side of the word to add a decorative brad. Peel off the backing and adhere to the bottom of the slide mount. Punch a hole through the tape and the mount at either end of the word, using a $1/16"$ (2mm) anywhere punch. Add brads through the holes. Before attaching the mount to the image, use scissors to notch out the areas of the image where the brads would hit, so the mount lies flat.

7. Adhere the image to the back of the mount using double-sided adhesive. Attach the mount to the cover of the book using craft glue. Repeat for the rest of the slides and images.

FOR THIS SLIDE BOOK, I USED THE PAPER SLIDES AS A FRAME TO CROP AWAY THE PARTS OF THE IMAGES THAT I DIDN'T WANT TO SHOW. I MADE THE BINGO "CHARMS" BY DRILLING A HOLE THROUGH EACH GAME PIECE. THE STAMPS FOR THE FACE IMAGES ARE FROM INVOKE ARTS; THE SCRIPT STAMP IS FROM STAMPOTIQUE.

JUDGING
BY THE COVER
(ALTERING VINTAGE BOOKS)

I'M ALWAYS COMING ACROSS OLD BOOKS, and a lot of them are disintegrating a bit, with the binding falling apart and the pages faded and worn. The best part of the book is the naturally aged cover, which is an ideal foundation for ephemera. If an old or rare book is not in excellent condition, it loses much intrinsic value; if you're worried about "destroying" a book that may have value, take it to a local used book dealer first to have it appraised.

hidden treasure

Old hardcover books are a cinch to find, and you'll have no trouble locating them at used book stores and antique malls, but you might want to make a local moving sale your first stop. Think about it: who wants to have to move a lot of books to their next house? Good deals are sure to be had!

I CHOSE THIS OLD BOOK FOR ITS DECORATIVE FRAME IMAGE PRINTED ON THE ORIGINAL COVER, KNOWING IT WOULD BE EASY TO ADD THINGS INSIDE THE BORDER. I ADDED AN HISPANIC RELIGIOUS ICON AND MILAGROS FOR A SHRINE EFFECT.

THIS BOOK WAS FALLING APART
WHEN I FOUND IT, SO I SPLIT
THE BINDING IN HALF AND USED
METAL REPAIR TAPE TO MAKE A
NEW BINDING. (THEY DON'T CALL
IT REPAIR TAPE FOR NOTHING!)
I FOUND THE RULER (ALREADY
BROKEN) AT AN ESTATE SALE AND
THE TABS ARE A COMBINATION OF
DYMO NUMBERS AND ELECTRIC
CAPACITORS. THE FRAME AROUND
THE IMAGE IS A VINTAGE BELT
BUCKLE; I REMOVED THE BAR TO
CREATE A FRAME FOR MY PHOTO.

TRUE BEAUTY
LIES WITHIN
(COLLAGING A THREE-DIMENSIONAL SHRINE)

BY DEFINITION, A SHRINE is a sacred or revered space. I tend to use the term more loosely and consider it a three-dimensional expression of collage—expression can be sacred, right? It is an engaging way to tell a story and offers much depth and space to work with, allowing you to use larger objects. Multiple surfaces allow for a more complex presentation. You can use a variety of containers to create shrines; my favorites are old wooden boxes and vintage cigar boxes.

BASIC NEEDS

- cigar box
- found or decorative paper (to cover box interior)
- double-sided adhesive
- alphabet stamps
- script stamp (STAMPOTIQUE)
- black inkpad (STAZON)
- gel medium
- foam brush
- cardstock
- Santos Paper Doll stamp set (INVOKE ARTS) (or figure stamp of your choice)
- foil stickers or other small stickers
- duster brush
- craft knife
- assorted beads
- 28-gauge annealed wire
- 1/16" (2mm) hole punch
- pencil
- additional collage elements (optional)

If you're not sure where to begin in assigning a theme to a shrine, think back to your childhood. Why not create a piece that honors a favorite memory? It doesn't have to be a big event. What about a favorite board game you used to love playing with a parent or sibling? If you don't still have the original game, check local thrift shops or try online with Ebay. Candy Land makes a comeback!

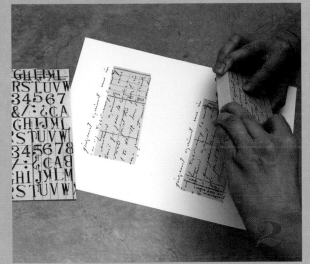

1. Layer pieces of paper to cover the inside bottom of the box. Tack the pieces together with double-sided adhesive but don't adhere them to the box yet.

2. Remove the paper you tacked together to make it easier to stamp or embellish. Here, I stamped alphabet letters repeatedly. Next, do the same thing for the sides of the box.

3. Brush gel medium over the entire interior of the box, with a foam brush. Adhere your stamped papers to the box, then coat the top of the paper with additional gel medium.

4. Set the box aside to dry. Stamp a figure to serve as your shrine subject onto cardstock. Here, I am using a Santos Paper Doll. If you would like to use embellishments such as these stars, and you don't want them to be so shiny, try dulling them a bit with a permanent inkpad and a duster brush. Hold them in place with the tip of a craft knife if you don't want to get your fingers inky.

5. After gluing in the distressed pieces, try adding beads to your main subject. 28-gauge wire works well to string them, and you can secure them to the bottom of your figure after punching holes in it with a 1/16" (2mm) hole punch.

6. Find the center of the top of the box and mark it with a pencil.

7. Pierce a hole at the mark using a craft knife. Glue a strip of paper horizontally at the top of the figure's head, on the back. Put glue on either end of the strip but not in the center area. Cut a length of wire and make a hook at one end by bending the wire. Insert the hook end through the strip of paper.

8. Insert the wire (with the figure hanging from it) through the hole at the top from the inside of the box to the outside. String one bead on the wire, punch a second hole close to the first hole with the craft knife and insert the wire back inside the box. Pull the wire taut and trim it if necessary.

9. Decide if your shrine needs any finishing elements and add those to finish. If you decide you don't want to display the box with the lid attached, remove it with a craft knife.

SOME SHRINES ARE SIMPLY A COLLECTION
OF REVERED ARTICLES, GATHERED IN ONE
PLACE FOR UNIFIED WORSHIP OR APPRE-
CIATION. OTHER SHRINES, SUCH AS THIS
ONE, ACTUALLY TELL A STORY. HOWEVER,
THAT STORY MAY BE OPEN TO INTERPRE-
TATION. . . THIS PIECE HAS A CERTAIN
CARNIVAL, FORTUNE-TELLING FEEL TO IT
THAT IS EXEMPLIFIED BY THE COLOR-OF-
NIGHT PAINT AND CELESTIAL STARS.

TO BE SEALED FOREVER

(ADHERING ELEMENTS WITH GEL MEDIUM)

GEL MEDIUM IS A CLEAR SEALER, adhesive and substrate all in one. It is available in a variety of thicknesses and a range of finishes from matte to high-gloss. Collage images are easily layered with this medium, which can go on clear over a background that is already painted or can be tinted for more of a layered effect. Gel medium receives rubber-stamped images easily as a final layer and allows for crisp and clean details. Oftentimes, it's even more accommodating than the naked paper itself.

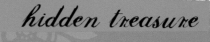

hidden treasure

Paper is perhaps the most obvious companion for gel medium, but what about fabric? Pieces cut from vintage aprons, linens or even upholstry can all be forever sealed in your collage work. Many times you can get an especially good price on vintage clothing because it is torn or damaged—what a great excuse to use it for collage! Immortalize your mother's hand-me-down kitchen towels by cutting out an image from them that you like and combine it with her favorite recipe for a warming tribute to her.

1. Begin with a piece of matboard as your surface. Choose a paper to use for the background, in this case, an old piece of sheet music. Coat the matboard with a generous amount of gel medium using a foam brush, and adhere the paper.

2. If the paper extends beyond the board, you can either fold it over or trim it off. Take a piece of tape, lightly press it on the paper and use it to remove some of the surface for a destressed look.

3. Rub the paper directly with a spongy inkpad like Ancient Page (pigment). Use as many colors as you like. (I usually use two or three.)

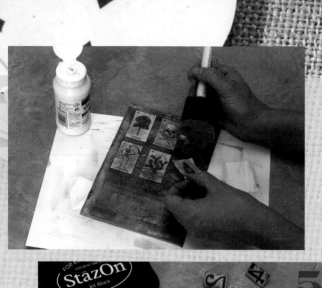

4. When you have the layers of color you are happy with, begin adding paper collage elements with a foam brush and gel medium. (I like to crumple up my papers first.)

5. After all of the elements are glued down, go over the board with another coat of gel medium. When it has dried, you can use permanent ink and rubber stamps to further decorate the surface.

crux de collage

For removing some of the surface of a paper to distress it, I like to use blue painter's tape because it's not so sticky that it takes off too much of the paper, but removes just enough to make the paper appear worn.

THE FRAME FOR THIS IMAGE IS ACTUALLY A PANEL FROM A 1920S HANGING LAMP. I DREW INSPIRATION FROM THE ARCHITECTURAL DETAILS OF THE COLUMNS AND ARCHES. I SEE MY SUBJECT LOOKING OUT THROUGH A WINDOW INTO A COURTYARD WITH STARS IN HER EYES AS SHE DAYDREAMS.

fly
away
little
bird
fly

HERE, I DREW INSPIRATION FROM OLD
SAILOR TATTOOS; SPECIFICALLY, ONE
THAT DEPICTED TWO BIRDS HOLDING A
BANNER WITH THE BELOVED'S NAME. I
KNOCKED OUT THE WINDOWS AND DOOR
PORTION OF THE SCHOOLHOUSE AND
ADDED A PICTURE OF MADDALENA, THIS
SCHOOLBOY'S LOST LOVE.

WHAT THE LAYERS REVEAL
(ADHERING ELEMENTS WITH BEESWAX)

MY FAVORITE TYPE OF COLLAGE to make combines melted beeswax with tailor's patterned tissue paper. I love the transparent, though slightly hazy, quality of the beeswax and the natural soft yellow color it offers. You can control the level of transparency by the amount of hot wax you add or remove. I like to work the printed tailor's marks on the pattern tissue into the composition. It creates a feeling of a story behind the image. Beeswax will accept rubber-stamped images, and you can use beeswax to adhere small, three-dimensional objects.

BASIC NEEDS

hot pot
(like a Crock-Pot)

beeswax

canvas board

foam brush

paint palette

acrylic paint, two colors
(one lighter, one darker)

paper towels

heat gun (optional)

patterned tissue
(such as a dress pattern)

craft brush

tape

quilting iron

paper collage elements

rubber stamps and inkpad
(optional)

hidden treasure

The women of today don't make their clothes as often as the two or three generations that preceeded them did. That doesn't mean the Butterick patterns that they used can't still be put to good use today—in creative collage work! If there's not a stockpile already in the drawers of your mother's sewing room (or she actually wants to keep using them!) check your local thrift store.

It's also fun to dress up blank gift tissue by typing on it with a typewriter, or stamping it with permanent ink.

1. Plug in your hot pot and fill it with beeswax, so it can begin melting. Start with either a canvas board or a piece of linen matboard. Use a foam brush to cover the board with the lighter-colored acrylic paint, then use paper towels to wipe and blot off a good deal of the paint. Add the darker color over the top of the first coat, but only in sections. Wipe off this color as well. Let the board dry thoroughly, or dry it with a heat gun.

2. Lay patterned tissue paper over your board where you want the pattern to be. Look for tissue that complements your composition. Using a craft brush, apply a layer of melted beeswax over the tissue. Cover the entire board.

3. Wrap excess tissue around the back of the board and secure with tape. Using a quilting iron, smooth the wax over the board to reveal more of the texture and the printing on the tissue. Scrape up the excess wax and put it back in the hot pot.

4. Remove as much or as little wax as you like. I like to remove most of the wax.

5. Cut out collage elements you want to add. Set an image on the board (it will stick naturally). Then brush over the element with beeswax.

6. Go back with the quilting iron and remove the excess wax. Be careful not to remove too much wax, or you may remove part of the image. If desired, burnish parts of the image with your fingers to make it shiny.

7. You can stamp on the wax also, if you like, using permanent ink.

crux de collage

Beeswax for crafting projects is available in brick, sheet and pellet forms. I prefer the pellets because it's easy to control how much I want to use.

When choosing a brush for beeswax collage, save your finer brushes and go for the flat bristle, wooden-handle variety. The brush can be used with the beeswax multiple times, but getting the wax out of the brush so you can use it for other projects is impossible. The brushes I use for this type of collage are never over a dollar each, and I don't feel bad when I have to throw one away.

Inexpensive Crock-Pots are sold at thrift stores. Whatever kind of hot pot you use, you will want to dedicate it to crafts only, and never again use it for food.

I USED AN OPTICAL LENS AND ITS M
TO ACCENT MY PRIMARY POINT OF
BEESWAX COLLAGE FEATURES A 19
OVER AN ASSORTMENT OF EARLY 1
TURE PLAYING CARDS. YOU COULD
DARD CARDS ON A COPIER TO CRE
EFFECT. STRATEGICALLY PLACED P
ADDS AN ADDITIONAL ELEMENT OF

FASHION FORTISSIMO

(HOME ACCESSORIES / JEWELRY / GIFTS)

WHETHER OR NOT YOU DECIDE TO WEAR YOUR HEART ON YOUR SLEEVE, I challenge you to at least wear your collage around your neck or on your wrist. Explore new heights in your creative endeavors, and wear them with pride! Wearable pieces of art are a joy to give to others, because when you've incorporated your personality, it makes it easy for the recipient to carry you with them always. For those who don't wear jewelry, it's still nice to make something you can't buy at a local department store (such as a collaged magnetic board). The projects in this section all have this uniqueness in common.

The thing I like best about these projects is that everyone can enjoy the result but each tells a story unique to the wearer. Every time someone asks, "Where did you get that necklace?", they can't believe I made it—that it is truly *handmade*—and they are just as fascinated to learn the stories behind the pictures.

Did you ever think you could collage a magnet board or a paperweight? In this section, we'll create collage pieces you can use and enjoy throughout your day—impressing everyone along the way!

HEART ON A STRING

(CREATING A DOMINO PENDANT WITH PAPER GLAZE)

I CAME UP WITH THIS IDEA AS A SOLDER-FREE ALTERNATIVE TO THE SLIDE PENDANT (page 100) for those times when I want a quick jewelry fix. It's an easy and inexpensive project to execute. Sometimes I use ball chain to hang the pendant and other times, leather cord. This is a small canvas, so consider reducing your images on the color copier and keep your text, if you have any, to a small point size. You can find predrilled dominos on the Internet or at your local stamp store. They make great gifts to commemorate a special occasion and great party favors too.

BASIC NEEDS

predrilled faux bone domino

found or decorative paper
  (for background)

pencil

scissors

craft glue

brayer

paper collage elements

black permanent maker

metallic leafing pen

nylon brush

paper glaze
  (ALEENE'S)

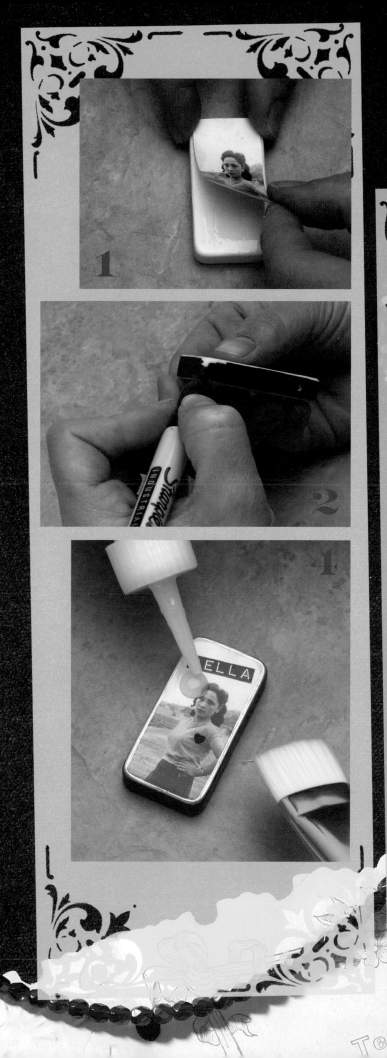

1. Start with a predrilled domino, or drill a hole in one yourself using either a drill press or a hand drill. Choose an image for the background of the collage, and trace the domino onto the portion of it that you wish to use. Cut out the shape with scissors, cutting it just a bit smaller than the traced line. The image should not extend past the bevel around the domino. Spread craft glue over the flat side of the domino and adhere the cutout image. Make sure you put the top of the image at the end of the domino that has the holes.

2. Use a brayer to smooth down the image and remove any bubbles. Add your individual collage elements. Avoid using elements thicker than cardstock weight. Next, use a black permanent marker to color in the sides of the domino.

3. Remove any excess glue coming out from behind the paper, then go over the bevel around the domino with a metallic leafing pen.

4. After the leafing has dried, use a nylon brush to cover the image with a coat of paper glaze. A light hand works best. You want the look to be smooth and free of brushstrokes. Add a second or third coat after the first coat has dried.

DOMINO NECKLACES TURN ORDINARY GAME PIECES INTO WEARABLE ART. YOU CAN APPLY THIS TECHNIQUE TO ANY FLAT SURFACE THAT WILL ACCEPT GLUED-ON IMAGES. THE DOMINOS USED HERE HAVE DOTS ON ONE SIDE, BUT THE BACKS ARE COMPLETELY BLANK. HOWEVER, YOU COULD TRY COLLAGING ON THE DOTS SIDE, INCORPORATING THE NUMBER OF DOTS INTO YOUR ART.

Oh dolce invito

IMMACOLATA CO... CIMINNA

Red Sky IN The Morning

A WOMAN'S HEART

CONSIDER MAKING A PENDANT THAT FEATURES THE IMAGE OF SOMEONE YOU LOVE, LIKE A FAMILY MEMBER, OR SOMEONE YOU GREATLY ADMIRE, SUCH AS AN AUTHOR OR A FAMOUS SAINT. YOU CAN USE SMALL WORDS TO TELL THE STORY OF THE PERSON, OR TO EXPRESS YOUR FEELINGS OF ADMIRATION. YOU MIGHT EVEN THINK ABOUT USING AN IMAGE OF YOURSELF, ALONG WITH A SAYING YOU'RE WELL-KNOWN FOR.

TINY TIN
(EXPLORING DIMENSIONAL COLLAGE IN A SMALL SPACE)

THIS IS A PROJECT THAT ANYONE CAN DO and feel proud of the result. The only supplies needed are glue, photos, small charms and other small treasures. The tins come in a variety of sizes and in boxes of multiples. It's fun to make a set or a series. I try to include at least three elements: a photo, some words and an object. These containers provide depth and dimension despite their tiny size. Trace the tin to determine the size of your photo, then trim your background photo just slightly within your traced circle pattern. First glue the trimmed image to the tin, then add other elements to complete the composition. You may wish to glue on the lid to protect the treasure inside. A round magnet is glued to the back with epoxy.

hidden treasure

When searching for tiny gems to include in small but dimensional pieces, don't forget about ordinary, less-decorative items. If a scrap of something helps illustrate your story—use it. Coffee beans, safety pins, worn or tarnished buttons, broken pieces of glass, toy parts that have fallen off the original toy . . . all things that you not only have lying around the house, but that appear completely different when displayed out of their normal context.

I LIKEN THESE COLLAGES TO SHRINES
IN MINIATURE. THEY REMIND ME OF
SMALL, INTIMATE DIORAMAS. USE INHER-
ITED TRINKETS FROM A LOVED ONE TO
HONOR A LITTLE SLICE OF HIS OR HER
LIFE. THE DEPTH OF THE TINS ALLOWS
YOU TO USE DIMENSIONAL OBJECTS TO
TELL YOUR STORY.

DESKTOP
DELIGHT
(COLLAGING ON AN UNEXPECTED SURFACE)

THE IDEA FOR COLLAGED PAPERWEIGHTS CAME FROM A DOMED GLASS PAPERWEIGHT I FOUND AT A THRIFT STORE. It was filled with dried flowers, but I thought it would be a nice way to display family photos—collage-style—on a desk. I found blank paperweights on the Internet (see Resources, pages 124–126); they come in a variety of sizes and shapes. The ones I use come with a foam insert you can discard and a cork bottom for a mounting surface. Use the cork as your template for your collage background. You can add photos, ephemera and shallow three-dimensional objects. Work in the same sequence as the Tiny Tin magnets to layer your elements. Once your collage is complete, add small drops of clear-drying glue to the very edge of the glass paperweight and adhere to the finished collage, so the edges of the cork and the glass paperweight meet. The thick glass acts as a magnifying glass that enhances the detail!

Another place you might not normally think to find collage is under a glass plate. Use paper glaze to adhere paper elements to the back of a clear plate, then display it on the wall with a plate hanger.

I CHOSE THIS HEART-SHAPED PAPERWEIGHT TO DEPICT THE LOVE MY FATHER LEFT ASHORE.

TI PENSO SEMPRE

hidden treasure

Small beads from vintage costume jewelry, old coins, game pieces, concert tickets, fortune cookie fortunes, torn pieces from old score cards . . . the list could go on forever, but you get the idea. Anything that can be glued down can be used in a dimensional collage. If you're working on a surface that must be flat, you can photograph or scan small items, cut them out, and still have a three-dimensional feel to a piece.

WHETHER YOU DECIDE TO SHOW-CASE YOUR OWN SACRED DEVOTION OR YOUR MOTHER'S DEVOTION TO HER WHEELS, THE MAGNIFICATION OF THESE PAPERWEIGHTS MULTI-PLIES THE FUN OF STANDARD TEXT AND TRINKETS.

MARBLE
MODA
(CREATING A COLLAGE MAGNET WITH EPOXY)

THIS IS ANOTHER SIMPLE PROJECT WITH A GREAT RESULT. Available in small and larger sizes, the marbles magnify the image and create a framed effect. It's a great way to display a single image, or you can create a series of these (think, "collaged magnetic poetry!") and use an altered Altoid tin as a gift box to give to a deserving friend. Look for marbles that have a flat side, rather than the type that are used exclusively for floral arrangements.

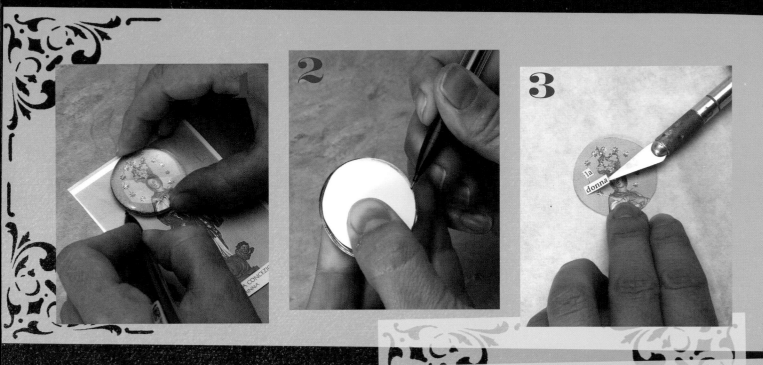

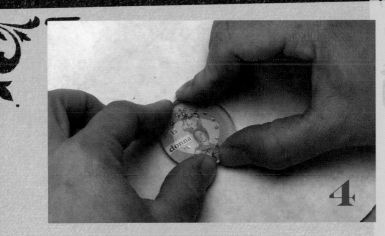

crux de collage

If you wish to have the look of Dymo lettering on your marble magnets, dominos or soldered jewelry, make a color copy of the punched-out text and use that instead of the actual plastic material.

1. Clean your marble with glass cleaner, if it needs it. Select an image to serve as the primary background, set the marble over the area of the image you wish to use and trace underneath the edge of the marble with a pencil.

2. Cut the traced shape out with scissors. After the image is cut out, set it back on the marble and mark with a pencil any areas that still need to be trimmed. Trim excess with scissors.

3. The image is now ready for collage. Use text-weight paper only for your elements. Set aside until you are sure the glue is dry.

4. Apply epoxy to the back of the marble and press firmly over the collage. Glue coming out of the sides is a good thing. Set aside to cure for several hours.

5. If globs of glue seeped out around the edges, wait until they are dry before trimming them off with a craft knife. Attach a magnet to the back of the marble, using E6000 and again, set aside to cure.

CHARMING
POSSIBILITY
(SOLDERING A MARBLE CHARM)

NOW THAT YOU'VE SEEN HOW EASY IT IS to use a glass marble as a collage carrier, marble charms are a good introduction to basic soldering. The surface area that receives the solder is large enough for you to get a good feel for the iron and not have to worry about keeping the flow in a straight line. This will allow you to get your technique down and become more familiar with the materials and the practice. I enjoy using the marble charms with vintage typewriter stickers because I can wear the words that express my passions.

BASIC NEEDS

waxed, parchment or freezer paper

glass marbles

stickers
  (the size of the marbles)

E6000 epoxy adhesive

18-gauge aluminum wire

round-nose pliers

hammer

metal block or anvil

¼" (6mm) black-backed copper tape

scissors

bone folder

craft knife

soldering iron
  (at least 30 watts)

flux (Sterling)

flux brush

self-clamping tweezers

Thin Ultimate or solid wire decorative solder

wet cloth or sponge

emery sanding block

paper towel or cotton swab

glass cleaner or acetone

1. Tear off a piece of waxed, parchment or freezer paper to work on. Select enough round stickers or, using a ½" (13mm) punch, punch out enough images to complete your necklace or bracelet. Select a sticker for each clear marble (or create a collage like the one on page 95). Apply epoxy to the flat side of one marble.

2. Set the glued side down on a sticker and press firmly. Repeat for each marble and set the marbles aside to cure.

3. To make a connector for a marble, start with a 2" (5cm) length of wire and bend the center into a U shape, using round-nosed pliers. Hammer the entire piece on an anvil or metal block, and make the ends especially flat.

4. Before foiling your marble, make sure it is clean and free of excess glue. Using the ¼" (6mm) copper tape, line the back of the marble with about three strips, overlapping the strips slightly.

97

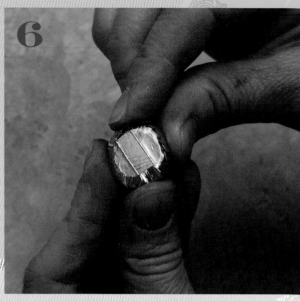

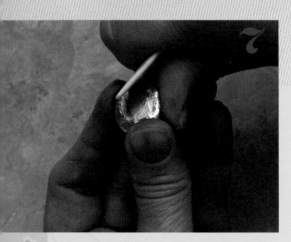

5. Trim around the marble to clean up the edges if necessary. Put a strip around the perimeter of the marble.

6. Use scissors to notch out the tape around the back where it overhangs the marble and fold over the tape all around the marble.

7. Burnish all of the tape well with a bone folder.

8. Use another piece of tape to secure the connector to the back of the marble. With the dull side of a craft knife, burnish around the wire.

9. Add another piece of tape over the ends of the connector. Burnish that too. If you're going to hang something from the bottom of the marble, add another connector to the bottom.

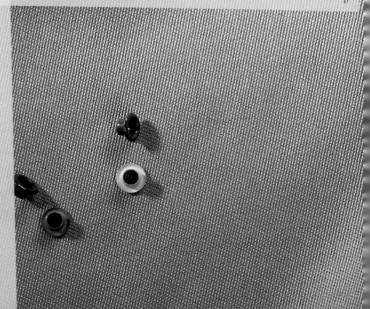

10. Plug in your soldering iron and let it heat thoroughly. Brush flux over the copper tape using the flux brush (it doesn't take much). The flux allows the solder to flow easily over the tape.

11. Secure the marble with self-clamping tweezers, in a position that will hold the marble still and level on your working surface. With the roll of solder in one hand and the iron in the other, melt a small glob of solder in the center of the back of the marble.

12. Take the iron and begin spreading out the solder to cover all of the foil. Periodically you should rub the tip of the iron over a wet towel or sponge to clean off the excess solder buildup. As you work on it, the piece will get very hot, so handle carefully. Continue smoothing out rough spots with the iron. A tapping motion with the iron works great — think of your iron as a brush.

13. When the piece is done and the marble has cooled, I like to polish the piece with a fine sanding block (manicure variety). If there are areas you aren't happy with, you can still go back and resolder them. Clean the finished marble with a paper towel and glass cleaner or a cotton swab and acetone.

TWO SIDES TO EVERY STORY

(CREATING A COLLAGE PENDANT WITH GLASS SLIDES)

OF ALL THE JEWELRY IN THIS BOOK, what I've coined "slide jewelry" is my favorite. It is two-sided, and you are not limited to using paper images to collage with. For instance, you can use ribbon or fabric as a background. Microscope slides offer similar sentiments as old-fashioned heart lockets. Wear one on a favorite chain or build your own chain and wear several at once (see page 112). I came up with the connector out of frustration when I could not easily solder a premade jump ring onto a slide. The connector allows for the construction of multitiered pieces. With the basic connectors and the jewelry findings that you'll explore on pages 106–109, you can create almost any design you wish. The influence for the larger pieces comes from my appreciation and growing collection of vintage jewelry over the past few years. Combining multiple slides provides yet another way to tell a story that is uniquely your own.

BASIC NEEDS

- piece of glass to cut down to size or two precut microscope slides
- black permanent marker
- cutting mat
- cork-backed ruler
- glass cutter
- found paper or image (for background)
- pencil
- scissors
- paper collage elements
- craft glue
- double-sided adhesive
- ¼" (6mm) black-backed copper tape
- bone folder
- 18-gauge aluminum wire
- round-nose pliers
- hammer
- metal block or anvil
- craft knife
- flux (Sterling)
- flux brush
- soldering iron (at least 30 watts)
- Thin Ultimate or solid wire decorative solder
- self-clamping tweezers
- wet cloth or sponge
- emery sanding block
- paper towel or cotton swab
- glass cleaner or acetone

As you're creating collages for slides, keep in mind that the metal tape that goes around the outside will cover up a little bit of the collage. Don't put anything too important at the edge.

1. If you are using glass other than a prepackaged slide, you will need to know how to cut it. Use a permanent marker to mark the glass where you want to make a cut. I like to cut glass on a cutting mat with a grid. Use a cork-backed ruler and set it far enough from the line that the cutting wheel is centered on the line.

2. Score with firm pressure down the length of the glass, then snap it to break it.

3. Choose an image to use for the background and trace the slide over it, using a pencil. I like to add some composition elements just to see how I will like the background.

4. Cut out the traced portion with scissors. Next, create your collage and glue down everything with craft glue. Small scrapbooking elements like paper flowers work well for little collages.

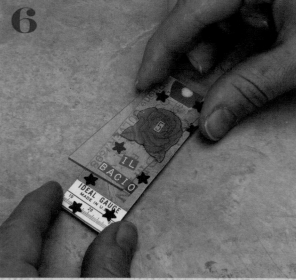

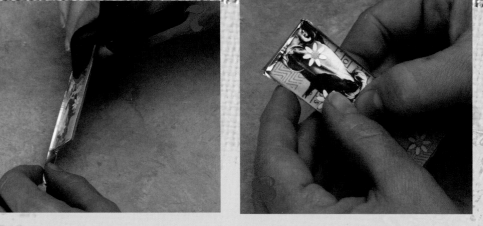

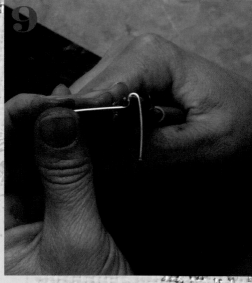

5. Make a total of two collages, one for each side of the slide. Label-maker tape will melt when the slide is soldered, but if you would like the appearance of the tape, make a color copy of it and use that instead.

6. Tape your collages back to back, using double-sided adhesive (just one spot is necessary). Clean the two glass pieces with glass cleaner and a paper towel, then sandwich the collages between the glass.

7. Roughly measure the perimeter of the slide, and tear off a length of metal tape measured accordingly. With the slides clamped together, wrap the tape around the slides, centering it over the seam. It doesn't really matter where on the slide you start the tape, just don't start it in a corner.

8. With scissors, notch the corners of the tape on both sides of the slide, then fold the tape over the slide.

9. Burnish the tape with a bone folder, going over both sides and the edge. To begin making a connector for the pendant, start with a 2" (5cm) length of wire. Hold the wire with round-nose pliers in the center of the wire and bend into a U shape. While still holding the wire with the pliers, bend one end up.

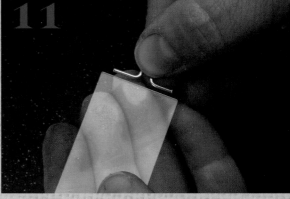

10. Bend the other end up to form a straight line with a U shape in the center.

11. Trim the ends so the total length is slightly shorter than the width of your slide.

12. Hammer the loop flat on both sides. Then, with the loop off the edge of the block, hammer the ends flat. If necessary, trim the ends of the wire, if they extend beyond the width of the glass sandwich, then re-hammer to remove any rough edges.

13. Here's the finished connector. Make connectors for as many sides of the slide as you will need to connect with. Be sure that the connector will sit level on the top of the glass.

14. Tape the connector to the top of the slide. (Tape one to the bottom and/or sides as well, if you are going to be connecting it with one or more other slides.) Notch the corners again, and fold the tape over the slide. Burnish around the wire with the dull side of a craft knife.

crux de collage

When cutting glass, sanding, soldering, cutting wire or hammering, it's good practice to wear safety glasses. You only have one pair of eyes, so protection is highly advised.

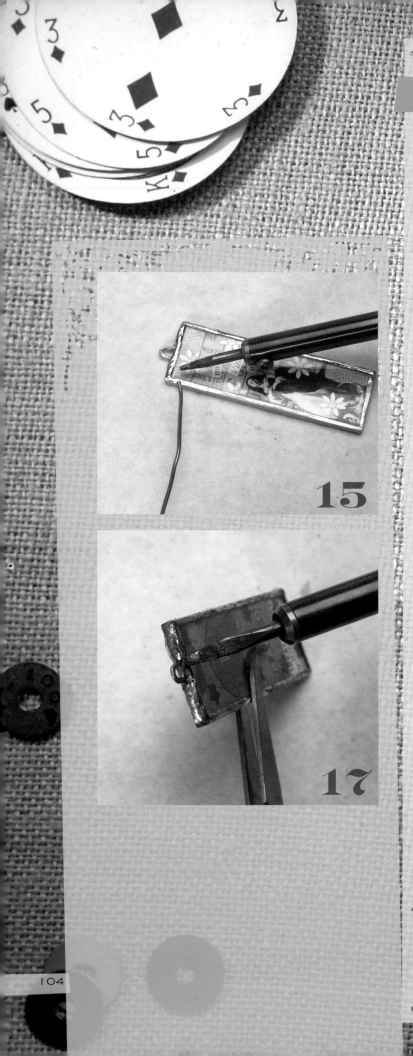

crux de collage

Don't worry about getting your solder to look perfect. It's OK to have bumps and imperfections. It you have a hard time getting the solder to adhere, try adding more flux.

15

16

17

15. Brush flux over the tape on the slide. Begin adding solder down the length of one side. Work with the iron on the inside (against the tape), the solder on the outside and run the two together around the edges.

16. After applying solder all the way around one side of the slide, let it cool, turn the slide over and then solder the other side. Let that cool, then solder the edge. Depending on how much solder you applied to the front and back, you may not need more for the sides, just spread it from what's already there, using a tapping motion. If, however, you like a chunkier look, add more solder from the roll.

17. For the side(s) with a connector use the self-clamping tweezers or a small vise to hold the slide for you. Work the solder around the wire, filling in any gaps or crevices. Sand with a fine block to finish. Clean the finished slide with a paper towel and glass cleaner or a cotton swab and acetone.

il fiore

la dolce vita

She's pretty all right

forever now let us kiss and part.

LA MANO

USING A FEW COMBINED ELEMENTS, SLIDE PENDANTS CAN TELL A STORY IN A SMALL SPACE BUT THESE PIECES ARE TWO-SIDED SO YOU CAN OFFER TWO SIDES TO THE STORY—TWO UNIQUE STATEMENTS IN A SINGLE CREATION! I WILL OFTEN DEPICT A SUBJECT'S PUBLIC SELF ON ONE SIDE OF THE PENDENT AND HIS OR HER INNER OR SECRET SELF ON THE OPPOSITE SIDE.

GENUINE
PARTS
(MAKING AND USING JEWELRY FINDINGS)

WITHOUT BEING LIMITED BY THE INVENTORY OF A JEWELRY-MAKING SUPPLIER, you can design your own necklaces and bracelets with these basic steps. The influence for these jewelry findings comes from hand-hammered silver vintage necklaces. Use these basic pieces in conjunction with the connectors to create tiered marble or microscope slide jewelry.

1. Cut 18-gauge aluminum wire into several 1½" (4cm) lengths. Make a mark with a permanent marker on your round-nose pliers that you will use as a guide for beginning each piece. Take one piece of wire and, with the end of the wire at the mark, roll it around completely.

2. Holding the loop firmly, bend it back to create the neck.

3. Repeat for the other end, rolling it in the opposite direction. Working on a metal block or anvil, hammer the link flat, on both sides.

LINKS

Experiment with different types of links; the ones shown here are only the basics. You may come up with designs that work better with your jewelry.

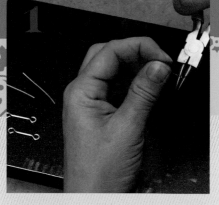

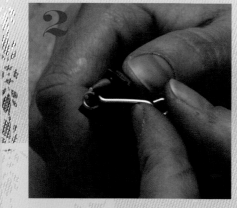

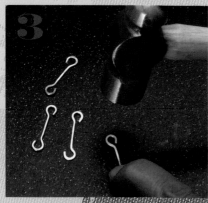

JUMP RINGS

Using this method, it's easy to create many jump rings at one time. These little rings are used together to create a chain, to connect links or clasps, or as spacers that allow the links to flow as a chain more easily.

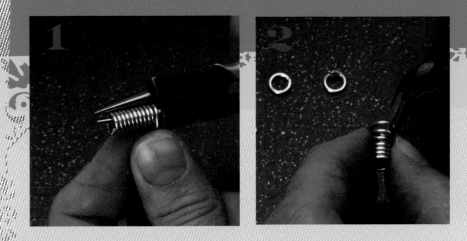

1. To create jump rings, make a coil from the wire. Grip the tip of the wire at the base of the pliers and rotate the pliers away from you. As you create the first circle, feed the wire directly below that circle and rotate the pliers in a back and forth motion, keeping the new wire at the base of the pliers.

2. Cut the coil from the roll of wire and spread it out just a bit so you can get your cutters between the coils. Cut apart after each rotation. Hammer the rings flat on a metal block or anvil.

HOOK CLASP

You can buy clasps in a variety of styles, but I think it's just as easy to make your own. In addition, by making the clasp out of the same wire as the links and jump rings, the finished look is cohesive and complete.

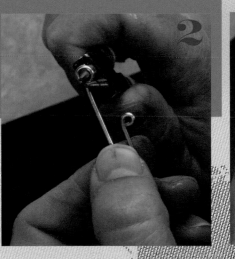

1. Cut a 2¼" (6cm) length of wire. Start with a tiny loop at one end, using the round-nose pliers. At about ¾" (19mm) from the tiny loop, bend the wire.

2. At the remaining end, form a loop at the mark on the pliers, then bend it back slightly to straighten out.

3. Cut another 2¼" (6cm) length of wire. At ½" (13mm) from the end, bend the wire, then bend the other end to meet it, forming an elongated link. Hammer both pieces flat on a metal block or anvil.

CREATING CHAINS

Infinite possibilities become available to you when you decide to make your own jewelry chain. Experiment with different combinations of links and jump rings. If you're feeling sassy, you may even add a bead now and then.

1. Several jump rings can be joined together to create a chain. Use needle-nose pliers to gently pry the rings open to join and squeeze closed to connect.

2. Join several links to make a chain, or use a jump ring to separate links.

3. Here are three chain examples: The top is shown with the addition of a hook clasp and jump rings separating the links; the middle chain is an example of using links without jump rings; the bottom chain is made solely from jump rings.

ASSEMBLING A NECKLACE

I always sketch out my designs on paper first; doing so is an easy way to determine what findings you will need and where the different connectors need to be attached to achieve the finished look you desire.

1. Start by making the chain that will go around your neck. There are several options here. You can make a chain of continuous jump rings, or you can combine the jump rings with links (see previous page). After the chain is complete, attach the center marble or slide using one jump ring.

2. Attach an equal number of marbles or slides to either side of the center one. Then attach another marble to the first (center) marble and continue connecting a symmetrical number of pieces from there—first left and right, then downward.

THREE WORDS I STRIVE TO LIVE BY.
EXPRESS YOUR OWN MOTTO IN YOUR
OWN WORDS. I CREATED THIS NECK-
LACE USING TYPEWRITER STICKERS BY
NOSTALGIQUES. THIS APPROACH ALSO
WORKS WELL AS A GIFT FOR A SPE-
CIAL MOTHER: DISPLAY THE NAMES (OR
PHOTOS) OF HER CHILDREN.

WHEN USING PAPER IMAGES AS YOUR BACKGROUND (AS I DID HERE WITH THIS SCRAP PAPER), TRY NOT TO OVERHEAT THE BACK OF THE MARBLE WHEN YOU ARE SOLDERING. THE EPOXY COULD BUBBLE AND SHOW THROUGH THE PAPER UNDERNEATH THE GLASS.

THE INFLUENCE FOR THIS NECKLACE COMES
FROM LAYERED VINTAGE JEWELRY. THIS IS A
GREAT WAY TO DEPICT A FAMILY TREE OR, IN
THIS CASE, I CHOSE RELIGIOUS ICONS AND
IMAGES FROM THE 1920s. THIS EXAMPLE
SHOWS HOW USING THE DIFFERENT JEW-
ELRY FINDINGS LETS YOU CREATE NUMEROUS
DESIGNS. FOR THE NECKLACE TO LIE FLAT,
AND TO LENGTHEN THE LAYERS, ADD SHORT
JUMP RING CHAINS BETWEEN THE TIERS.

DON'T LIMIT YOURSELF TO WORDS OR IMAGES
ALONE. I USED COLORFUL PIECES OF FABRIC
FOR THE BACK SIDES OF THESE SLIDES. YOU
CAN ALSO EXPLORE OTHER SIZES OF GLASS
IN ADDITION TO THE STANDARD MICROSCOPE
VARIETY. THE CONTRAST BETWEEN THE TINY
SQUARES AND THE THREE LONG PIECES IS
WHAT REALLY SETS THIS PIECE APART. YOU
CAN USE TEXT ON THE FIRST TIER TO TELL THE
STORY OF THE IMAGES ON THE BOTTOM TIER.

IS ANOTHER VARIATION OF HOW
AN APPLY THE DIFFERENT FIND-
TO CREATE OTHER JEWELRY PIEC-
UCH AS BRACELETS TO MATCH OR
EMENT YOUR NECKLACES. BRACE-
E IS EASY TO ADJUST WHEN YOU
MP RINGS AND YOUR OWN LINKS.

A PREFERENCE FOR LEATHER

(COMBINING SOLDERED PIECES WITH LEATHER)

LEATHER IS ANOTHER MATERIAL YOU CAN USE IN CONJUNCTION with the microscope slides. The charms on this bracelet are sewn onto the leather band for a more casual look, and the colored thread adds a hint of interest. You could even add charms to a vintage leather handbag for a one-of-a-kind look, or how about embellishing a thrift store belt? The striking contrast between leather and glass is sure to catch second glances wherever you roam.

BASIC NEEDS

black leather remnant

craft knife

ruler

cutting mat

hammer

1/8" (3mm) anywhere punch

1/16" (2mm) anywhere punch

1/16" (2mm) eyelets, ten

eyelet setter

1" x 1/2" (2cm x 13mm) collaged and soldered slides, five (see pages 100–105)

needle

colored thread

craft glue

ENLARGE THIS DIAGRAM 133% TO BRING TO ACTUAL SIZE

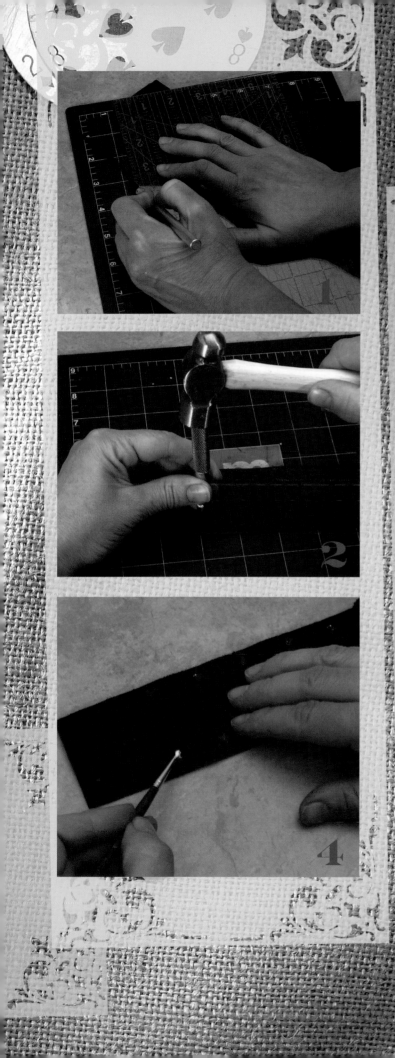

1. These dimensions work for a bracelet that uses five 1" x ½" (2cm x 13mm) slides. Cut a piece of black leather to about 2" x 7½" (5cm x 19cm). I like to use a craft knife, ruler and cutting mat to trim it. Also, cut a strip of leather that is about ¼" wide by 8" (6mm x 20cm) to tie the bracelet.

2. Refer to the diagram on the opposite page for measurements, then use a hammer and a ⅛" (3mm) anywhere punch to make eight holes that will be used for the adjustable bracelet tie (two holes on one end, and six holes on the opposite end. Then, find the center of the band to start the remaining holes, and use the ¹⁄₁₆" (2mm) punch to make two rows according to the diagram (twenty total, for attaching the slide pieces).

3. Set ¹⁄₁₆" (2mm) eyelets in the ten small outer holes, using a ¹⁄₁₆" (2mm) eyelet setter. Thread a needle with four strands of thread. Beginning in the center, sew the slides to the leather. Pass through the holes about three times.

4. Tie a knot in the back, trim the thread, then secure the knot with a dab of craft glue.

MAGNETIC ATTRACTION

(COLLAGING ONTO SHEET METAL)

THE INFLUENCE FOR THE MAGNET BOARD CAME FROM SOMETHING I saw in a catalog for posting messages and memos. This is another good project for practicing your soldering, as it uses a larger surface for mastering the technique. When you are not using the magnet board for your messages, it's a unique alternative to traditional framing. Instead of collaging with vintage images, as I did here, you may want to use current family photos, or mementos from a romantic vacation.

BASIC NEEDS

½" (13mm) circular stickers or ½" (13mm) circle punch and images to punch out

½" (19mm) superstrong magnets

craft glue

paper glaze

nylon brush

galvanized sheet metal
  (cut to desired size)

glass
  (cut to the same size as the sheet metal)

paper collage elements

double-sided adhesive

³/₈" (10mm) copper tape

bone folder

18-gauge aluminum wire

round-nose pliers

hammer

craft knife

flux (Sterling)

flux brush

soldering iron
  (at least 30 watts)

locking pliers

Thin Ultimate or solid wire decorative solder

wet cloth or sponge

emery sanding block

paper towel or cotton swab

glass cleaner or acetone

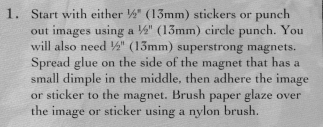

WHILE THE PROJECTS SHOWN ON THESE PAGES ARE VERY OBLONG IN THEIR PROPORTIONS, THIS TECHNIQUE WORKS JUST AS WELL IN MORE STANDARD OR SQUARE SIZES. ONE ADVANTAGE TO LONG AND NARROW: IT'S AN EASY SOLUTION FOR A TOUGH-TO-FILL WALL SPACE.

1. Start with either ½" (13mm) stickers or punch out images using a ½" (13mm) circle punch. You will also need ½" (13mm) superstrong magnets. Spread glue on the side of the magnet that has a small dimple in the middle, then adhere the image or sticker to the magnet. Brush paper glaze over the image or sticker using a nylon brush.

2. Create a collage to fit the size of the galvanized sheet metal, and cut a correspondingly sized piece of glass. Follow the directions for foiling and soldering the Slide Pendant (steps 7–17, pages 102–104) to complete the board. The magnets will adhere to the metal through the glass.

crux de collage

For a horizontal board, make a connec-tor for each end; for a vertical board, just make one for the top. The board can hang from the connector itelf.

COLLAGE CLIPPINGS

WHAT ONCE WAS LOST IS NOW FOUND, right here, ready for you to use in your own creations. Have fun with the images on these pages and give them a second life in lovely works of art.

Box 333
Pedro Miguel
Canal Zone.

GREETINGS
U.S. FRIGATE CONSTITUTION
"OLD IRONSIDES"

Miss Lounica Wyman
Cherokee
North Carolina

#138
Pedro Miguel
Canal Zone

Save
envelope for
me, it may be
worth money later on

CRISTOBAL-MIAMI
INAUGURATING
33 HOUR
SCHEDULE
F.A.M. 5
MAY 1 1930

Miss Lounica Wyman
Concho
Oklahoma

VIA AIR MAIL

Box 197
Pedro Miguel
Canal Zone

VIA AIR MAIL

Miss Lounica Wyman
1402 E. Elm
West Frankfort
Illinois.

Dated *Jan 4th* 188**8**

George McAulay

—TO—

Donald McLeod

Chattel Mortgage

TO SECURE THE SUM OF

$ 6641⁰⁰

Due Dec 19th 1888

Newsome & Leyden, Law Stationers, 46 Adelaide St. East, Toronto.

*Select in the County
Court on the 5th day
of Jan 1888 by
William Gunn*

8	23	38	53	68
9	24	39	54	69
10	25	40	55	70
11	26	41	56	71
12	27	42	57	72
13	28	43	58	73
14	29	44	59	74
15	30	45	60	75

RESOURCES

GENERAL SUPPLIES
Most supplies are available at your local stamp, craft, hardware or art stores, but if you have trouble locating an item, contact the manufacturer directly for retail information.

ACE
www.acehardware.com
metal repair tape

AMERICAN TOMBOW, INC.
www.tombowusa.com
tombow mono adhesive

DIANE RIBBON AND NOTIONS
www.dianeribbon.com
super-strong magnets

DUNCAN ENTERPRISES
www.duncancrafts.com
aleene's tacky glue • aleene's paper glaze

HEAVEN SENT INSPIRATIONS
www.craftercity.com
paperweights

VENTURE TAPE
www.venturetape.com
copper foil tape

COLLAGE SHEETS AND MATERIALS
Each source offers a unique selection of supplies and collage materials. I encourage you to explore each company and find materials that interest you.

ARTCHIX STUDIO
www.artchixstudio.com
collage sheets

BEADS GALORE INTERNATIONAL INC.
www.beadsgalore.com
beads

COLLAGE STUFF
www.collagestuff.com
wide assortment of collage materials

DOVER PUBLICATIONS
www.doverpublications.com
copyright-free clip art books

EK SUCCESS LTD.
www.eksuccess.com
jolee's by you flowers • rebecca sower— nostalgiques stickers

A LITTLE BIZAAR
www.alittlebizaar.net
collage sheets

PAPER HOUSE PRODUCTIONS
www.paperhouseproductions.com
stickers

PAPER REFLECTIONS, DMD INC.
www.dmdind.com
collage packs • assorted papers

MELANIE SAGE
www.melaniesage.com
collage sheets

SILVERCROW CREATIONS
www.silvercrowcreations.com
small bottles • capacitors • rusty screen

SNAPATORIUM
www.snapatorium.com
old photos

STAMPDIVA
www.stampdiva.com
gold paper wings

STAMPOTIQUE ORIGINALS
www.stampotique.com
tintype collage sheet • microscope slides

TUSCAN ROSE
www.tuscanrose.com
collage sheets

PAPERS

CAVALLINI AND CO. PAPERS
www.cavallini.com

DAISY D'S PAPER COMPANY
www.daisydspaper.com

DESIGN ORIGINALS
www.d-originals.com

K & COMPANY
www.kandcompany.com

7 GYPSIES
www.sevengypsies.com

TOOLS

DYMO CORPORATION
www.dymo.com
dymo label makers

FISKARS
www.fiskars.com
decorative punches • scissors

MAKING MEMORIES
www.makingmemories.com
wire cutters • self-clamping pliers • basic tool kit

STAMPINGTON & COMPANY
www.stampington.com
metal letter stamps

JUDIKINS
www.judikins.com
duster (stipple) brushes

RUBBER STAMPS AND INKPADS

CATSLIFE PRESS
www.catslifepress.com
rubber stamps

CLEARSNAP, INC.
www.clearsnap.com
ancient page inkpads

INVOKE ARTS
www.invokearts.com
rubber stamps

THE MOON ROSE ART STAMPS
www.themoonroseartstamps.com
rubber stamps

PSX DESIGNS
www.psxdesigns.com
rubber stamps

RANGER INDUSTRIES, INC.
www.rangerink.com
tim holtz–distress ink • embossing powders

STAMPINGTON & COMPANY
www.stampington.com
rubber stamps

STAMPOTIQUE ORIGINALS
www.stampotique.com
rubber stamps

TSUKINEKO, INC.
www.tsukineko.com
stazon inkpads • versafine inkpads

UPTOWN RUBBER STAMPS
www.uptownrubberstamps.com
rubber stamps

If you ever find yourself in my hometown of Phoenix, Arizona, I encourage you to visit the following stores:

STAMPOTIQUE ORIGINALS
9822 N. 7th St., #7
Phoenix, AZ 85020
602-862-0237
www.stampotique.com

DIANE RIBBON AND NOTIONS
2319 W. Holly St.
Phoenix, AZ 85009
800-622-7263
www.dianeribbon.com

SAGE ANTIQUES
335 W. McDowell Rd.
Phoenix, AZ 85003
602-258-3033

QCUMBERZ
4429 N. 7th Ave
Phoenix, AZ 85013
602-277-5133

BEADS GALORE
3320 S. Priest Dr. #3
Tempe, AZ 85282
800-424-9577
www.beadsgalore.com

INDEX

METAL CRAFT DISCOVERY WORKSHOP

by Linda & Opie O'Brien

Discover a nontraditional approach to the introduction of working with metal and create twenty fun and funky projects. This is the whimsical side of metal that teaches you how to cut and join metal surfaces and also allows you to explore ways to age and add texture to metal, conjure up beautiful patina finishes and put to use numerous types of metal such as copper, mesh, wire and recycled material. Whether you've worked with metal before or you're new to the medium, give your recyled tin cans a second glance and start crafting beautiful pieces with metal today.

ISBN 1-58180-646-9, ISBN13 978-1-58180-646-5
paperback 128 pages, 33255

COLLAGE DISCOVERY WORKSHOP: BEYOND THE UNEXPECTED

by Claudine Hellmuth

In a followup to her first workshop book, Claudine Hellmuth taps into a whole new level of creativity in Beyond the Unexpected. Inside you'll find original artwork and inventive ideas that show you how to personalize your own collage pieces using new techniques and interesting surfaces. In addition, the extensive gallery compiled by Claudine and other top collage artists will spark your imagination. Whether you're a beginner or a collage veteran, you'll enjoy this lovely book both as inspiration and as a practical guide.

ISBN 1-58180-678-7, ISBN13 978-1-58180-678-6
paperback 128 pages, 33267

ART STAMPING WORKSHOP

by Gloria Page

Create a signature look with stamped images you carve yourself! Art Stamping Workshop introduces you to the world of carving and printing soft blocks to create great gifts, home décor items and personal apparel—all with a look uniquely yours. Detailed instructions on carving tools and techniques get you started. Then you'll learn to create twenty projects on paper, fabric and alternative surfaces, such as wood and polymer clay. Templates for re-creating all featured stamp designs are included as well. Carving your own stamps gives you the freedom to use any image at any size and sets your work apart from the crowd. Discover the fulfillment that comes from printing your own images and start carving your stamps today!

ISBN 1-58180-696-5, ISBN13 978-1-58180-696-0
paperback 128 pages, 33355

VISUAL CHRONICLES: THE NO-FEAR GUIDE TO ART JOURNALS, CREATIVE MANIFESTOS & ALTERED BOOKS

by Linda Woods & Karen Dinino

Have you always wanted to dive into art journaling, but you're always stopped by what to put on the page? Finally, there is a book that comes to your rescue! Visual Chronicles is your no-fear guide to expressing your deepest self with words as art and artful words. You'll learn quick ways to chronicle your thoughts with painting, stamping, collaging and writing. Friendly projects like the Personal Palette and the Mini Prompt Journal make starting easy. You'll also find inspiration for experimenting with colors, shapes, ephemera, communicating styles, symbols and more!

ISBN 1-58180-770-8, ISBN13 978-1-58180-770-7
paperback 128 pages, 33442

THESE BOOKS AND OTHER FINE NORTH LIGHT TITLES ARE AVAILABLE FROM YOUR LOCAL ART & CRAFT RETAILER, BOOKSTORE OR ONLINE SUPPLIER.